CW01372306

ON LAND, AT SEA, AND IN THE AIR

PALITOY REGD
ACTION
man
ACTION SOLDIER
by PALITOY
the movable fighting man
Move him into ACTION POSITIONS
PALITOY REGD
ACTION
man
ACTION PILOT
by PALITOY
This box contains your Action Man dressed like this
The movable fighting man!
PALITOY REGD
ACTION
man
ACTION SAILOR
by PALITOY
This box contains your Action Man dressed like this
The movable fighting man!

ON LAND, AT SEA, AND IN THE AIR

N.G. TAYLOR

The author would like to thank Hasbro for creating the *Action Man* concept and toys and for allowing him to use the *Action Man* trade mark and reproduce the copyright in *Action Man* products and packaging throughout the book.

Action Man products and packaging © 1966-2003 Hasbro. Used with permission.

First published in the UK by New Cavendish Books in 2003

Copyright © 2003 New Cavendish Books

All rights reserved. No part of this book may be reproduced or transmitted in any form or by any means, electronic or including photocopy, recording or any other information storage and retrieval system, without prior permission in writing from the publisher.

Publisher: Narisa Chakra
Photography: Neil Taylor
Design: Olivia Koerfer

ISBN: 1 872727 99 9

Printed and bound in Thailand by Amarin Printing & Publishing (Plc) Co. Ltd.

New Cavendish Books
3 Denbigh Road
London W11 2SJ
Tel: 020 7229 6765
Fax: 020 7792 0027
email: narisa@newcavendishbooks.co.uk
www.newcavendishbooks.co.uk

CONTENTS

		Introduction	9
LAND	1	Action Soldier	12
	2	Combat & Bivouac	14
	3	Command Post	16
	4	Military Police	18
	5	Army Medic	20
	6	Ski Patrol & Mountain Troops	24
	7	Beachhead Assault	26
SEA	8	Action Sailor	30
	9	Navy Attack	32
	10	Navy Dress Parade	34
	11	Navy Frogman – Underwater Demolition	36
AIR	12	Action Pilot	40
	13	Scramble	42
	14	Survival	44
	15	Air Police	46
SOLDIERS OF THE CENTURY	16	German Stormtrooper	50
	17	Russian Infantryman	54
	18	French Resistance Fighter	56
	19	British Infantryman	58
	20	Australian Jungle Fighter	60
	21	American Green Beret	64
THE SECOND WAVE	22	Bazooka	68
	23	Mine Detection Set	70
	24	Landing Signal Officer	72
	25	Crash Crew Set	74
	26	Commander	76
	27	Infantry Support Weapons	78
	28	Armoured Car Commander	80
	29	Sabotage	82
	30	Combat Engineer	84
	31	Red Devil Parachutist	86
	32	Breeches Buoy Rescue Set	88
	33	Royal Canadian Mounted Police	90
SPORTSMEN & EXPLORERS	34	Olympic Champion	94
	35	Cricketer	96
	36	Footballer	98
	37	Judo	100
	38	Jungle Explorer	102
	39	Mountaineer	106
	40	Adventurers	109
	41	Polar Explorer	110
	42	Underwater Explorer	114

CEREMONIALS

43	Grenadier Guardsmen	118
44	Argyll & Sutherland Highlander	120
45	Life Guard	122
46	The Blues & Royals	124
47	17th / 21st Lancer	126
48	Royal Marine – Dress Uniform No 3	128
49	Royal Hussar	130

REGIMENTALS

50	Parachute Regiment	134
51	Royal Marine	136
52	Royal Marine, Mountain & Arctic	138
53	Royal Marine Exploration Team	140
54	British Army Officer	142
55	Royal Military Police	144
56	Dispatch Rider	146

SOLDIERS OF THE WORLD

57	French Foreign Legionnaire	150
58	Late Issue German Stormtrooper	154
59	"Colditz" German Stormtrooper	156
60	Late Issue German Infantryman	158
61	Late Issue Russian Infantryman	160
62	Late Issue British Infantryman	162
63	Late Issue Australian Jungle Fighters	164
64	Mine Detection	166
65	Last Issue Mountain & Arctic Uniform	168
66	Late Issue Parachute Regiment	170
67	Late Issue Royal Marine	172
68	Late Issue Royal Military Police	174
69	Late Issue Tank Commanders	176
70	Late Issue Medic	178
71	Last Issue Medic	180

INTERNATIONALS

72	Deutsches Afrika Korps	184
73	Russian Infantryman	188
74	German Paratrooper	190
75	US Paratrooper	192
76	2US Marine	194
77	Helicopter Pilot	196
78	United Nations Soldier	198

THE OFFICERS

79	RAF Battle Of Britain Pilot	202
80	Luftwaffe Pilot	204
81	Panzer Captain	206
82	Camp Kommandant	208
83	Escape Officer	210
84	British Army Major	212
85	Late Issue British Army Major	214
86	SAS Officer	216

THE SPECIALISTS

87	Commando	220
88	Royal Engineers	222
89	Long Range Desert Group	224
90	SAS Commander	226
91	SAS Secret Mission Pod & Assault Craft	228
92	SAS Frogman	230
93	SAS Paratrooper	232
94	Fireman	234
95	Police Patrolman	236

THE BEST OF THE REST

96	Sailor	240
97	Raf Working Dress	242
98	Field Training Excercise	244
99	Tom Stone Uniform	245
100	British Infantryman	246
101	US Machine gunner	248
102	7.62MM GP	250
103	Lewis Gun	252
104	General Electric Six-Pak Minigun	254
105	Russian Kalishnikov PK	256
106	SIG 510 - 4	258
107	Late Issue Poncho	260
108	Second Issue Combat Jacket	262
109	Late Issue Camouflage	263
110	Assault Craft	264
111	High Rescue	266
112	Late Issue M-3	268
113	Underground Rescue	270
114	Highway Hazard	272
115	27th Cavalry	274

Author's Note:

Throughout this book various plastic derivatives have been described and are categorised as follows:

Plastic – hard material used to mould First Issue helmets, rifles, knives, and radios;
Polyurethane – more substantial than PVC, but more pliable than plastic and used for straps, ceremonial cartouche boxes, berets and later issue helmets: and
PVC – used to mould some types of leather belt, field telephone covers, tubing and machete sheaths.

OFFICIAL EQUIPMENT MANUAL

PALITOY REGD
ACTION man

The movable fighting man

Kit out your Action Man for every phase of military service with these authentic true-scale equipment sets.

COLLECT 21 ACTION MAN STARS AND GET ANOTHER ACTION MAN FREE!

Once you have bought your first Action Man you can start collecting Action Man stars. You will find one, two, three, four, or five stars on every equipment set. Cut them out and paste them on the special Star Card enclosed with every Action Man figure. When it is full (21 stars) post it to Bakelite Xylonite Limited, Toy Division, Owen Street, Coalville, Leicester together with 2/- P.O. to cover post and packing. You will receive an *undressed* Action Man free. (So you can kit him out in your own Soldier, Sailor or Airman Outfits.)

ACTION man BOOKS

Exciting Military, Sport and Adventure books show how Action Mans Equipment is used in real life.

STAR SCHEME

There are stars on most pieces of Action Man equipment. Once you have bought your first Action Man you can start collecting them. Cut them out and paste them on the special Star card enclosed with every Action Man figure until you have enough for the item you choose, then send them to Palitoy Ltd., Coalville, Leicester, together with a postal order to cover the cost of postage and packing.

Action Man (undressed) send 21 stars and 13 p. P.O.
Mountie Uniform send 18 stars and 10 p. P.O.
Guard Dog send 10 stars and 10 p. P.O.

palitoy
Palitoy Limited

ON LAND, AT SEA, AND IN THE AIR

Anyone who is interested in Action Man will no doubt be able to remember the first time they were given, or bought, one. In my case it was an Action Soldier on holiday in Weymouth in 1966 after seeing this revolutionary toy being previewed on "Blue Peter".

The purpose of this book is not to produce a dry and sterile reproduction of the manuals of uniforms and equipment, much less a thorough display of every Action Man figure or uniform released. So there are few vehicles, and no deep sea diver or any of the later spacemen for example. My collection is focused unashamedly on the military outfits produced for the "best equipped, most realistic model fighting man the world's ever seen - almost a foot tall with 20 moveable parts". Action Man was first introduced into Britain in 1966 by Cascelloid, a division of Bakelite Xylonite Ltd of Owen Street, Coalville, Leicester under license from the American firm Hassenfeld Brothers (HasBro) of Pawtucket, Rhode Island, where GI Joe had already hit the beach two years earlier. The photographs try and show the figures in realistic and lifelike settings. As an Action Man fan first, and a photographer second, the objective has been to achieve a lifelike pose for the figure to show off the details on the uniforms to best advantage.

During my primary Action Man period 1966 - 1975, I used to take photos of my figures with the sort of results you'd expect, matchstick sized men in all sorts of improbable situations. During the second phase, 1990 to date, the objective has been to illustrate prime examples of the uniforms in the sort of conditions you'd expect to see a real wearer in. The photographs have been taken over a number of years in a variety of locations which hopefully underline the theme of this book which has also matured over a period of time. This collection of photos has led to some risk, some humour and a lot of patience from my wife who has seen me disappear for hours whilst new locations were checked out and guns carefully put in place. Reverse shots are also illustrated, like the best military uniform books, to show off the equipment that would otherwise be obscured from view. Not every piece of equipment for each set is shown on some occasions and although my collection is extensive it does not include every piece. For those of you who find this irritating I apologise.

As most avid collectors will know Action Man and his compatriots had various "issues" of uniforms with the First Issue generally being the best quality. Where possible First Issue gear has been used although some items were only available in later period quality issues. Similarly I only have used the First Issue type of painted head figures as in my view the later flock haired eagle eye figures were not so realistic with their more orange skin colouring. Having said that the fixed hands have proved a challenge as few of the weapons can be held (at all?) and look natural.

Having set out the rationale for the theme of this book I hope you will enjoy looking at the detail of each photograph. It's dedicated to my son, Miles who doesn't really know what he's missing!

N.G. TAYLOR 2003

OUTDOOR COMBAT AREAS YOU CAN BUILD FOR YOUR "ACTION MAN", ACTION SOLD...

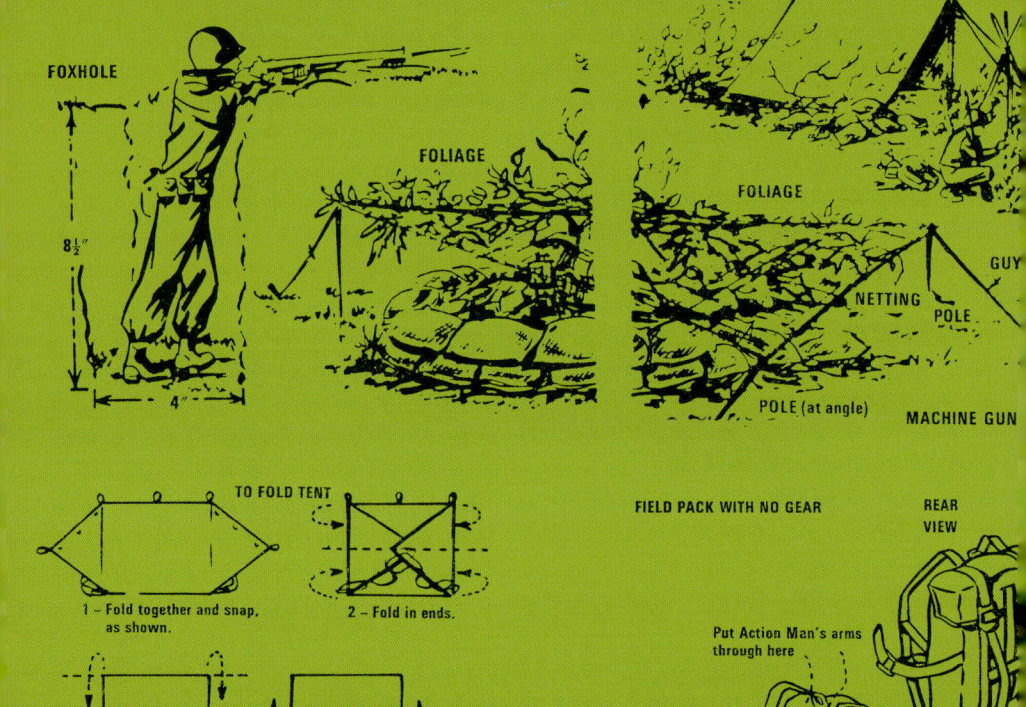

FOXHOLE
8½"
4"

FOLIAGE

BIVO...

FOLIAGE

NETTING

GUY
POLE

POLE (at angle)

MACHINE GUN

TO FOLD TENT
1 – Fold together and snap, as shown. 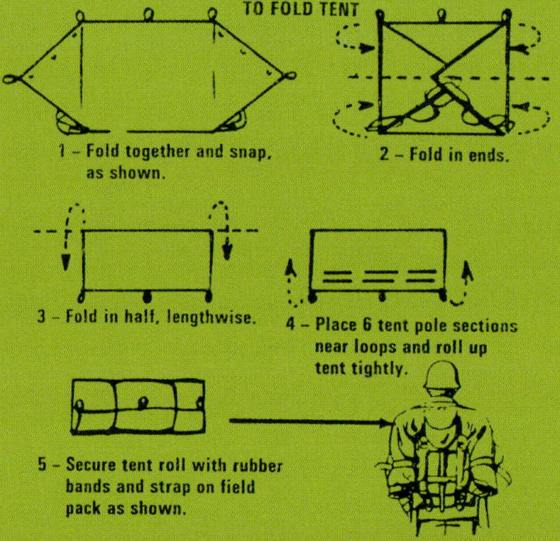
2 – Fold in ends.
3 – Fold in half, lengthwise.
4 – Place 6 tent pole sections near loops and roll up tent tightly.
5 – Secure tent roll with rubber bands and strap on field pack as shown.

FIELD PACK WITH NO GEAR

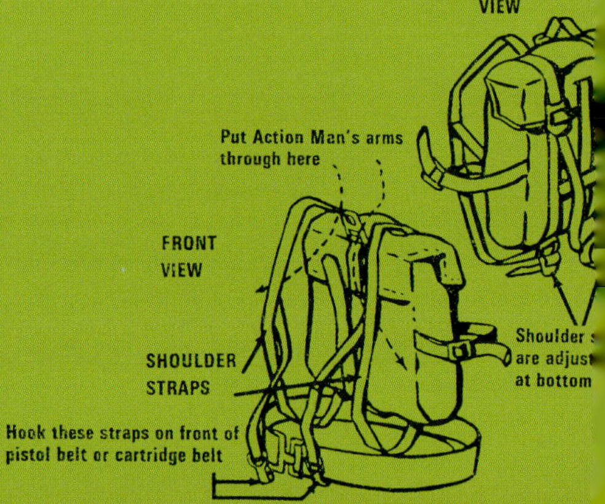

REAR VIEW

Put Action Man's arms through here

FRONT VIEW

SHOULDER STRAPS

Shoulder s... are adjus... at bottom

Hook these straps on front of pistol belt or cartridge belt

INSTRUCTIONS FOR ASSEMBLING TENT

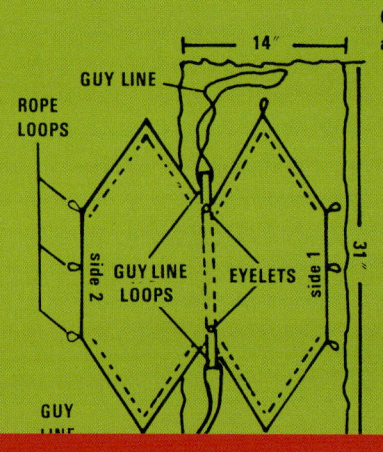

Contains 6 tent pole sections and 10 tent pegs.

GUY LINE
ROPE LOOPS
14"
31"
side 1
side 2
GUY LINE LOOPS
EYELETS
GUY LINE

1 – Cut a piece of corrugated cardboard 14" x 31" to use as base for setting up tent.
2 – Lay tent flat on cardboard with two guy line loops on top (see illustration). Make sure side 1 of tent is about one inch from edge of board.
3 – Put a peg through each of 3 rope loops at side 1 of tent and fasten by inserting peg into board. (If this is difficult, pre-punch board with pencil).
4 – Join 3 of the 6 pieces of tent pole sections to form a tent pole by inserting plugs into tent pole

5 – Insert small end of tent pole into underside of either eyelet and stand tent pole straight up. This raises one end of tent.
6 – Keeping pole straight, put a peg through the rope loop nearest pole on side 2 of tent and fasten by inserting peg into board. Draw guy line nearest pole taut and fasten with peg.
7 – Repeat steps 5 and 6 for other end.
8 – Insert pegs in remaining loop of side 2 and flap loops at each end.

TENT CAMOUFLA...
6 insert plugs
6 tent pole sectio...
10 tent pegs

10

LAND

PLATES 1-7

Kit out your Action Man for every phase of military service with these authentic true-scale equipment sets.

1. ACTION SOLDIER

QUARTERMASTER

- green kepi
- denim shirt
- denim trousers
- brown boots
- embossed metal identity tag
- Army Training Manual, cream cover, serial number AM 93530000
- equipment manual

Dressed in regulation cut denims, kepi and brown boots the Action Soldier represents the basic US Army recruit. He came complete with embossed metal identity tag, 'Action Man by Palitoy', an equipment manual and cream covered Army Training Manual, serial number AM 93530000, which was effectively the catalogue number.

All basic Action Soldiers, Sailors and Pilots were unarmed and only issued with the basic kit described in the relevant section.

SPECIAL FEATURES

Shirt
Shirt - square breast pockets, no epaulettes or cuffs. Two buttons on the main seam with two further buttons on the rectangular flap of each pocket. The ribbon label on the inside collar was marked Palitoy, Action Man, Made In Hongkong and there were six bullet holes through the words 'action' and 'man

Trousers
Trousers – double stitched waist hem, two rear open square pockets, with one or two poppers at the front. There were no other matching Combat trousers you could buy separately and you had to get the Action Soldier if you wanted to embark on a set of army equipment until two years later when an equipment card of the fatigues, without the boots, was available.

Kepi
Kepi - green polyurethane with no manufacturer's marks, the peak has six rows of moulded stitching on it, and a seam on the back.

Boots
Boots – brown polyurethane. The moulding was supposed to represent the eight eyelet combat boot that was used by the US during the World War Two/ Korea era. Boots were important in 1966 as they only came with the basic Action Soldier, Sailor or Pilot figures. Apart from the Ski Patrol Set, boots were not available separately unless you collected 21 equipment stars and sent off for a red haired undressed Action Man who arrived with another pair of high brown boots and a dog tag. Only blonde or dark haired basic soldier, sailor and pilot figures were available in the high stree

1. ACTION SOLDIER

2.1

2. COMBAT & BIVOUAC

QUARTERMASTER

- Combat field jacket
- eight pouch cartridge belt
- M1 rifle
- bayonet
- grenades
- Combat field pack
- entrenching tool
- canteen and cover (see 7. Beachhead Assault Set)
- mess kit, knife, fork, spoon
- first aid pouch
- Bivouac Sleeping Bag
- Bivouac 'De Luxe' Pup Tent, including poles, connecting pins, and pegs
- Camouflage netting and foliage
- Browning .30 calibre machine gun (see 9. Navy Attack)
- ammunition box (see 100. US Machine Gunner)

Separate Equipment Card:
- A1 helmet
- camouflage netting
- foliage

Separate Equipment Card:
- camouflage netting
- foliage
- tent poles and connecting pins

NOT SHOWN – .30 calibre machine gun, tripod, ammunition box, canteen and cover (see Plates 7.2, 7.4 and 9.4.)

SPECIAL FEATURES

Combat Field Jacket
These Plates illustrate the premier quality of the combat jacket, which has a zip front with poppered button cuffs, buttons on each epaulette and an internal green waist draw cord. The jacket has two square breast pockets with pointed flaps and two pointed flap hip pockets. Plates 2.1 and 2.2 show the quality of the material, and the double stitched hem and cuff detail.

Field Pack
All the equipment is packed according to the Army Training Manual, with the posts and pegs of the tent rolled inside the tent canvas. Inside the pack itself went the sleeping bag and the mess kit with knife, fork, and spoon. At the base of this pack is the rolled camouflage netting for the tent. When the full compliment of equipment is stowed into the pack it is extremely cumbersome in relation to the figure. Plate 2.3 shows the complete field pack with the rolled pup tent fastened by the three straps, plus the green plastic entrenching tool in its poppered thick weave cloth cover.

Bayonet
The silver plastic bayonet is moulded to fit the two types of First Issue infantry weapon, the M1.30 Garand semi automatic rifle and the M1.30 carbine. It was available in the main Field Jacket Set and on two separate equipment cards.

Pup Tent
The olive green Bivouac deluxe Pup Tent is finished to a high standard with two guy ropes, six pole sections and ten distinctive pegs and ties. Three plastic pole sections are fitted together with wire pins and slotted into an eyelet at the end of both ridges. There are three sets of poppers on each end flap, which allow the tent to be fully opened. Plates 2.4 and 2.5 illustrate the tent pitched. Guy ropes are looped through separate ties at each end of the tent and fastened with a cream polyurethane peg.

At each side of the tent are a further three eyelets with individual ties threaded through to help peg the tent down and a further tie at the end of each tent flap. Over the top of the canvas is draped camouflage netting and polyurethane foliage in different colours issued with this Set, the Combat Helmet and the Combat Camouflage Netting Set equipment cards.

The tent has no groundsheet and is big enough inside to fit the sleeping bag, the top of which can just be seen in Plate 2.5, alongside the extended trenching tool.

Entrenching Tool
The green plastic entrenching tool is made from four different parts – handle, shovel head, screw fastener and collar. By loosening the collar the shovel head can be fastened and folded back onto the handle.

2. COMBAT & BIVOUAC

Adding to the basic fatigues the Combat Soldier is equipped with an eight pouch cartridge belt for the hard brown plastic M1 rifle (extensively used in World War Two by the US forces) with a green six cord elastic strap.
Each belt is made from double folded heavy weave material, with three rows of stitching and two metal fasteners. The girth can be adjusted using a polyurethane rectangular loop which matches the colour of the three first types of First Issue belts – white (MP/Navy/Ski Patrol), sand (pistol belts) and green (cartridge belts).

3. COMMAND POST CAPE SET

QUARTERMASTER

- hooded cape
- field telephone with case
- wire roll
- field radio
- Colt .45 pistol
- black holster
- sand pistol belt
- map and case

SPECIAL FEATURES

Map Case
A silver map case with stencilled 'MAPS' legend and circular Hasbro ® inscription on the base. The ubiquitous map sets out details of the airstrip, pond, farm and some unidentified buildings in the vicinity of this firebase. Plate 3.1 shows a communications bunker made using the Combat Camouflage Netting Set. Note the tent pole sections being used to hold up the netting.

The camouflaged uniform in this Plate is a Second Issue version, indicated by the fact that it has only pointed-flap breast pockets on the tunic.

Cape
Advancing in his waterproofed cape, this GI carries the wire roll and chestnut brown field telephone. The cape fastens together with two poppers on each side of the body and there are also draw cords at the base of the hood. This First Issue piece is a cumbersome article as the waterproofing material makes it difficult to roll the cape tightly enough to fasten into the base of the field pack in the required manner.

Field Radio
Shown in the carrying position in Plate 3.3, the field radio has green six-cord elastic shoulder straps. The aerial here is extended and the black handset is attached to the body of the radio by its clip (the field telephone handset does not have one). There is a Hasbro ® inscription on the base of the radio at the back and also inside the inner moulded casing, which is subdivided with a slot for the telephone handset when not in use. The wire roll has copper wire looped around a central green plastic drum and a moveable handle.

NOT SHOWN – sand coloured pistol belt, pistol or holster (see Plates 4.3 and 21.2.)

TO FOLD CAPE
Place cape face down and fold back, as shown
Fold down.
Fold over.
Roll up.
Complete. Attach to bottom of field pack, as shown.

3. COMMAND POST CAPE SET

3.1

4. MILITARY POLICE

QUARTERMASTER

- 'Ike' tunic
- trousers
- white pistol belt
- Colt .45 pistol
- black holster
- wood coloured truncheon
- red neck scarf
- MP armband
- kitbag

Separate Equipment Cards:
- white A1 helmet, pistol belt, Colt .45, holster, truncheon
- jacket, scarf and armband
- trousers
- kit bag

On guard duty at the gates of a secured area, these Plates highlight the quality of the detail on this set.

SPECIAL FEATURES

Kit Bag
When full, the kit bag is fastened by linking a wire hook on the strap to a thin wire loop threaded through the four eyelets. Note the square shaped base to the bag.

Uniform
This Set includes an open necked, waist length 'Ike' tunic with two back darts and three poppers. It has rounded and pleated breast pockets with pointed flaps, epaulettes, a two tier medal ribbon and two buttons on the rear of the waistband. The matching trousers have a single rear pointed flap pocket on the wearer's left.

Equipment
Also included are a white triple stitched pistol belt, a Colt M1911 A1.45 moulded in steel grey plastic with a brown pistol grip, a black holster with fastener and orange PVC thigh strap, a wood coloured plastic truncheon with an orange strap, poppered red dress neck scarf and the kitbag. The navy blue armband is made of felt with a stencilled yellow MP legend, and fastens with a hook and eye sewn on the inside.

The white A1 'snowdrop' helmet with the black stencilled legend 'M.P.' was only available on a separate equipment card.

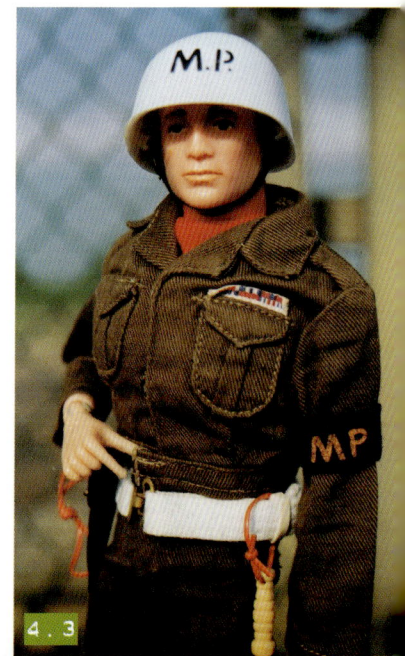

4.2

4.3

18

4. MILITARY POLICE

4.1

5. ARMY MEDIC

QUARTERMASTER

- stretcher
- red cross flag
- red cross armband
- medic bag
  CONTENTS:
  - rolled gauze bandage
  - triangular gauze bandage
  - plasma bottle
  - stethoscope
  - four plastic splints
  - small safety pins

Separate Equipment Card:
- A1 helmet with Red Cross insignia

Overleaf the Medic holds a rolled gauze bandage whilst the plasma bottle is attached to the wounded figure's M1 rifle. These four Plates show the use of the basic Combat Soldier fatigues as a base for the equipment from this Set.

SPECIAL FEATURES

Plasma bottle
The transparent plastic plasma bottle is made in two parts, the top has a triangular wire clip and there is a black gauge on the blood red paper insert. At the bottom of the clear tubing is a pin that can be inserted into a patient's clothing.

'Unit One' Medic Bag
This is made of the same heavy weave material as the Combat Field Pack and the entrenching tool cover. The double stitched shoulder strap is connected to the bag itself by a semi-circular hook buckle and ring on either side. The bag fastens with a single popper sewn to a strap at the bag's front.

Helmet and armbands
The A1 helmet was only available from a separate equipment card and has white circular Red Cross insignia on both sides. The white felt armbands also have a Red Cross emblem. Note the white centre to the cross in each case. Seen in Plate 5.4 is a GI Joe A1 helmet, in a light green camouflage.

If the 5" x 3.75" flag has a solid red cross, rather than the original white centred type shown on the helmet and armbands, it is a later issue piece.

Stretcher and equipment
The advancing stretcher party of Plate 5.2 illustrates the green plastic riveted V braces fastened to the legs in each corner of the stretcher; these braces could be drawn together for storage when not in use. The stretcher comprises ten green plastic parts plus a 10.5" x 4" canvas panel. Pins on the stretcher legs penetrate the canvas and are fixed into the arms of the stretcher. This piece and the flag were only available in the main Medic Set.

Shown overleaf, in Plate 5.4, are both the crutch and the grey PVC tubed stethoscope included in this set, together with a selection of wood coloured plastic splints. The splints come in two sizes: 2.5" and 3.5", and two of each are provided in the Set together with some small safety pins to fasten the bandages.

20

5. ARMY MEDIC

5.1

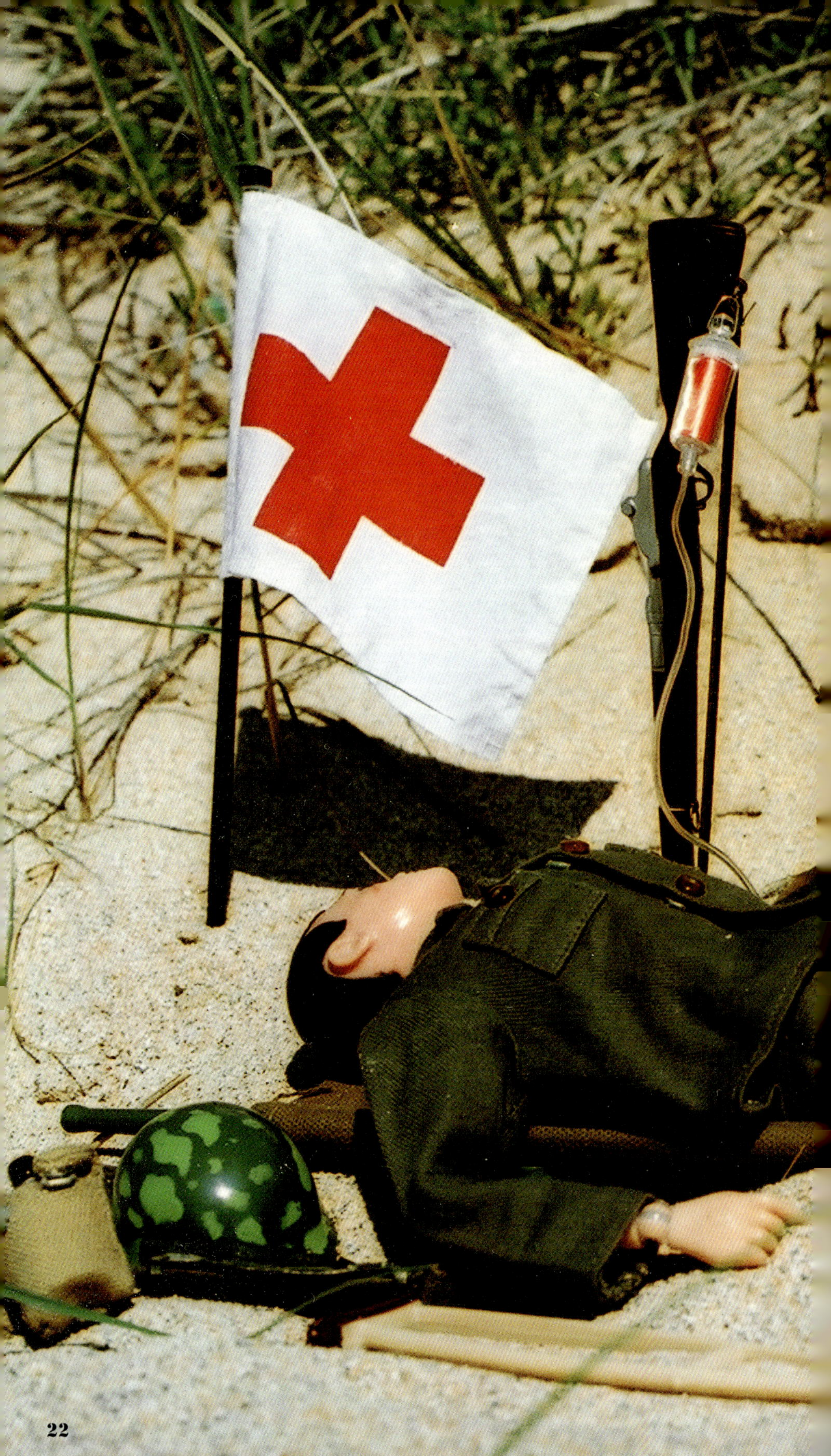

5. ARMY MEDIC

5.4

6. SKI PATROL

QUARTERMASTER

SKI PATROL
- hooded parka
- trousers
- mittens
- goggles
- black ski boots
- skis
- ski poles

MOUNTAIN TROOPS
- white field pack
- white pistol belt
- ice axe
- snowshoes
- climbing rope
- grenades

Separate Equipment Card:
- white A1 helmet and insignia
- white eight pouch cartridge belt
- white M1 rifle
- grenades

SPECIAL FEATURES

Parka
The close up detail of the parka, right, shows the circular insignia on a separate breast badge and the diagonal pointed flap pockets. The Parka is fastened with two poppers and two or three draw cords – at the hood and skirt hem and, in early versions, also at the waist. The trousers have draw cords at the waist with a single popper, cuffs are elasticated at wrist and ankle. The rear view of the Trooper in Plate 6.4 illustrates the back of the parka, made in two parts with a centre seam and cut to a fish tail design with draw cords.

The white cartridge belt is similar to the green Combat piece with two sets of four pouches. These open and are fastened with gold painted polyurethane hooks; they are threaded over the belt with rectangular loops at the rear of each pouch section.

Skis and Ski Poles
The white plastic skis are inscribed Hasbro ® Japan, and have three grooves on the underside. Also inscribed Hasbro ® Japan are the two part moulded ski sticks – poles with painted black handles and orange PVC straps, and circular end sections with silver painted spikes.

In actual arctic conditions, Plate 6.3 shows the Trooper on skis. They are attached to the four-eyelet black ankle ski boot by a figure of eight wire and a metal footplate with four protruding tabs.

Goggles and Mittens
The green plastic goggles have a black four-cord elastic strap and can be distinguished from later models, or reproductions, by a white painted edge running around the whole outline of the eyepiece (later versions are not painted around the nose V). The mittens are elasticated at the wrist and cut to a separate thumb pattern.

Field Pack and accessories
Plate 6.4 also shows the heavy weave of the material used in the Mountain Troops field pack. This pack has seven silver buckles instead of the brass versions used in the green Combat piece. The vivid yellow climbing rope was only available initially in the Mountain Troops Set.
The white M1 rifle was the same mould as the brown Combat version but with black instead of silver metal parts. There are three rings attached to the loops on the butt and barrel and a Hasbro ® inscription at the end of the butt. The ice pick also has a brass ring attached to the base of the silver painted axe head.

Also shown is the lattice moulding at the top of the polyurethane snowshoe.

A trooper is shown wearing the two piece full winter white camouflage suit, helmet, goggles, and mittens with skis and poles. The white helmet has the blue circle, star and roaring bear insignia.

6. SKI PATROL

7. BEACHHEAD ASSAULT

QUARTERMASTER

Four separate equipment cards:
- camouflaged assault jungle tunic
- camouflaged assault jungle trousers
- flame thrower
- paratrooper small arms

Also shown:
- GI Joe A1 light green camouflage helmet
- GI Joe jungle camouflage Pup Tent, (not available in Britain)
- GI Joe jungle camouflage poncho, (not available in Britain)

SPECIAL FEATURES

Flame-thrower and Small arms
This side view of the flame-thrower in Plate 7.1 shows the main tanks mounted on a black base plate with two black six cord elastic straps. There is an inverted Hasbro ® inscription on the base of the plate. A separate pressure tank is held in place between the two fuel tanks by a brass clip. The silver plastic, two handled gun has a Hasbro HongKong inscription and is connected to the base of the tanks by black PVC tubing (see also Plate 20.2). Note the detail of the grain on the uniform cloth.

Beachhead Assault Uniform
On patrol in full jungle camouflage uniform, Plate 7.2 illustrates the full set, with knife and scabbard shown attached to the left leg. The plain green A1 helmet has the nylon camouflage netting attached (with a black single-cord elastic hoop at the net's opening fitted under the helmet rim). The jacket and trousers are in the same style as the basic Action Soldier denims, but of thicker material.

The M1.30 Carbine has a green six cord elastic strap fixed with a brass ring at the base of the barrel and a pin and slot arrangement on the butt. This model of the actual weapon held 15 rounds in its curved magazine. Plate 7.3 provides better detail of the M1.30 with bayonet and Mk2 A1 grenades.

The Mk2 A1 'pineapple' grenades were common to several Action Man equipment sets, in bags of four or six. After World War One the Americans started to produce this model from an original French design. The grooves in the grenade's casing were designed to fragment.

U.S. Marine Camouflage
Plate 7.4 illustrates the GI Joe camouflaged helmet, pup tent and rolled poncho, which also has the Marine jungle camouflage design. These camouflaged items were not available in Britain as they formed part of a distinct US Action Marine Set only issued in America.

NOT SHOWN – Parachute Pack (see Plate 13.4)

26

7. BEACHHEAD ASSAULT

7.1

28

SEA

PLATES 8-11

8. ACTION SAILOR

QUARTERMASTER

- white naval cap
- light blue denim work shirt
- dark blue denim trousers
- black ankle length boots
- embossed metal identity tag
- Navy Training Manual, dark blue cover, serial number AM 94132220
- equipment manual

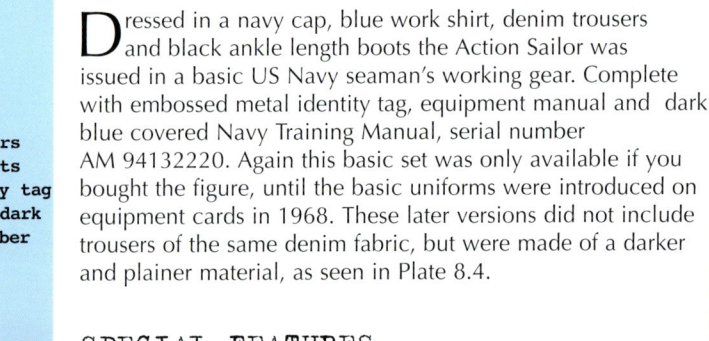

Dressed in a navy cap, blue work shirt, denim trousers and black ankle length boots the Action Sailor was issued in a basic US Navy seaman's working gear. Complete with embossed metal identity tag, equipment manual and dark blue covered Navy Training Manual, serial number AM 94132220. Again this basic set was only available if you bought the figure, until the basic uniforms were introduced on equipment cards in 1968. These later versions did not include trousers of the same denim fabric, but were made of a darker and plainer material, as seen in Plate 8.4.

SPECIAL FEATURES

Shirt
Light blue denim, poppered cuffs and three main poppers, the shirt has three light blue buttons on the double sewn front seam. On the left breast is an ope pocket with a pointed base and hem. Plate 8.2 shows the separate shoulder yoke section.

Trousers
Fastened by two poppers, the dark blue denim trouser is cut in a bell bottomed style with two pointed open pockets just below the waist at the front

Cap
Made of white polyurethane, the crown was moulded with six triangular sections within which there were "stitched" triangles. Plate 8.3 shows the heavy weave pattern on the side. There is a Hongkong inscription at the cent of the inside crown.

The white cotton US Navy kit bag shown was only available in the GI Joe rang

NOT SHOWN –
Identity Tag

30

8. ACTION SAILOR

8.1

9. NAVY ATTACK

QUARTERMASTER

- orange life jacket
- red and yellow signal flags
- signal lamp
- binoculars

Separate Equipment Card :
- Browning M1919A4 .30 machine gun
- navy blue ammo box

Separate Equipment Card:
- navy A1 helmet
- signal lamp
- binoculars

Separate Equipment Card:
- life jacket

SPECIAL FEATURES

Life Jacket
The orange kapok filled life jacket is made from four main sections - a back, two front pieces and the high collar. There are three sets of white ribbon ties at the front of the jacket, the lowest being sewn all around the body.

Signal Flags and Helmet
The signal flags are made from two unhemmed diagonal pieces of red and yellow material singly stitched and attached to the wood coloured plastic shafts by a sewn overlap. The flags were only available with the main Set until the range was expanded in 1968/69. The Navy Attack Set was then deleted, and replaced by two equipment cards. Plate 9.4 is a close up of the life jacket and the black signal lamp with the yellow paper lens. The Navy A1 helmet was based on the same mould as the green Army type - a single moulding for the shell, with two separate lugs on either side of the temple, connected by a black four-cord elastic strap and buckle. Hasbro ® is inscribed inside, with a mould number.

Machine Gun and Tripod
The navy machine gun was the Browning .30 M1919A4 with its M2 Mounting Tripod – the standard US infantry support weapon. The piece shown here is the same as that included in the Action Soldier Bivouac Set. There are three versions of this piece – the First Issue silver plastic one illustrated here, a similar model in black plastic and a final black version with fixed tripod (see Plate 100.1).

The tripod is made of six components – the front leg and mounting plate, two longer rear legs, and a metal adjustment brace with two circular ribbed sleeves that slide up and down the rear legs. These moveable legs are riveted to the mounting plate. A separate plastic cradle connects the gun to the tripod with two clips either side of the body of the gun and a central pin that fits into the mounting plate. All these parts allow the piece to be set in a variety of positions. Plate 9.1 shows the legs folded.

The gun itself is moulded in two halves, with a black painted handle and muzzle. As this weapon was originally air-cooled there are four sets of nine holes in the barrel. The navy blue ammo box with its white stencilled lettering is another piece made up of several components: the main body, diagonally sided top, and rectangular handle with two brass clips.

Binoculars
Around the neck of the figure in Plate 9.1 are the standard Action Man First Issue black binoculars. These are made from two half moulds, with flat eye and lens pieces, and a single cord of black elastic threaded through the top of each side of the piece.

9. NAVY ATTACK

9.3

9.1

10. NAVY DRESS PARADE

QUARTERMASTER

- white M1 rifle
- white pouch belt
- bayonet
- white truncheon

Unlike the GI Joe range there was no separate Action Man Shore Patrol Set (as illustrated on the Action Sailor box). All the pieces in this set are similar to their Army counterparts and would have been used by naval personnel in any land based operations or security duties.

SPECIAL FEATURES

The Navy Dress Parade equipment card supplied the Action Sailor with a white M1 rifle and pouch belt, bayonet and white truncheon (not shown, see Plate 15.3.)

Note the shape of the trouser hip pocket, which is clearly outlined in this Plate, and the adjustable belt loop.

10.2

10.1

34

10. NAVY DRESS PARADE

11. NAVY FROGMAN SET
UNDERWATER DEMOLITION

QUARTERMASTER

- trousers
- top
- headpiece
- orange polyurethane face mask
- diver's depth gauge
- knife and scabbard
- three sticks of orange plastic dynamite
- flippers
- air cylinders

The three piece black rubber suit has a pair of trousers, top and headpiece. There is no stitching apart from around the zip of the top. Plate 11.1 shows the set in full, complete with orange polyurethane facemask, diver's watch, knife and scabbard, and orange plastic dynamite.

SPECIAL FEATURES

Dynamite
The three sticks of orange plastic dynamite were originally only available in the main set and not on any equipment card. The dynamite is made in two parts – the top, with blue painted fuses, and a hollow moulded plastic orange body tube.

Accessories
The scabbard attaches to the leg with loop ties, at the top made from black four-cord elastic and the bottom from a single elastic cord. The facemask has a clear plastic lens. The diver's watch is a moulded circular clip of black plastic with a yellow paper sticker face. Black polyurethane flippers form a complete shoe for each foot and are inscribed Hasbro ®. Plate 11.2 provides a clear view of the facemask, flippers, knife handle and scabbard loop ties.

Air Cylinders
Unlike the flame thrower tanks the Frogman's air cylinders are not connected together with moulded plastic rods but are glued separately onto the black base plate. The circular air valve is stuck into holes at the top of each cylinder and connected to the black plastic mouthpiece by two orange PVC tubes. The black six-cord elastic straps thread through the baseplate and are joined with a pinched brass clasp. The side view of the air cylinders in Plate 11.1 shows part of the black base plate, which is common to the flamethrower (see Plate 7.1

11.2

11. NAVY FROGMAN SET

11.1

AIR
PLATES 12-15

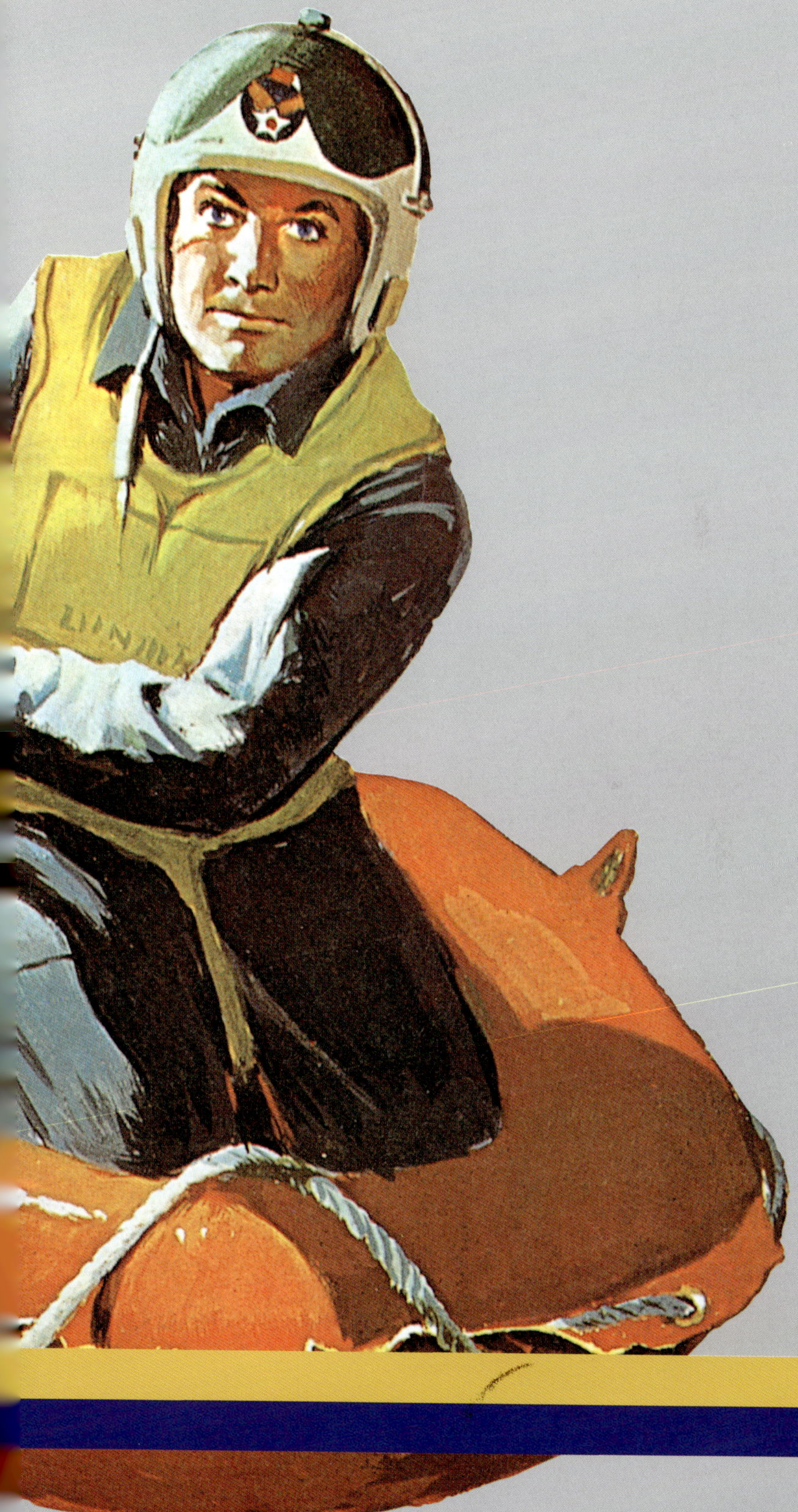

12. ACTION PILOT

QUARTERMASTER

- blue kepi
- orange working overalls
- black boots
- embossed metal identity tag
- Air Force Training Manual, grey cover, serial number AM 9381110
- equipment manual

Dressed in zippered working clothes, blue kepi and black boots this Action Pilot figure represents a USAF groundcrew member complete with embossed metal identity tag, equipment manual and Air Force Training Manual serial number AM 9381110.

SPECIAL FEATURES

Boiler Suit
An orange one piece work suit with zip front, and elasticated cuffs. The suit has a simple one piece collar, and no epaulettes or pockets. This pattern was the original for all subsequent one piece suits. A rear view in Plate 12.2 shows the two vertical side pleats and the elasticated half waist.

Clipboard
The clipboard, paper and working red leaded pencil only came with the First Issue Scramble Set and the Action Pilot's Communications equipment card. A black six-cord elastic strap, shown around the wrist of the figure in Plate 12.1, is used to secure the pad to the thigh of the Scramble Pilot.

Kepi
The same pattern as the Action Soldier's, the kepi is made of blue polyurethane with moulded peak stitching and no manufacturer's marks.

Boots
The high black polyurethane eight-eyelet boots are again based on the same pattern as the Action Soldier's.

40

12. ACTION PILOT

12.1

13. SCRAMBLE

QUARTERMASTER

- flight suit
- life vest
- pistol belt
- Colt .45
- holster
- clipboard, pad and pencil

Separate Equipment Card:
- parachute pack

Separate Equipment Card:
- Scramble crash helmet

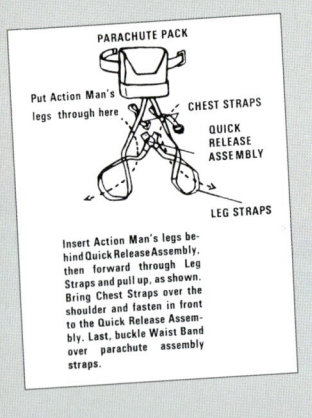

The Action Pilot in full Scramble gear including all the accessories

SPECIAL FEATURES

Flight Suit
The grey one piece zippered flight suit uses different shades of material for different parts of the suit, in this instance the poppered cuffs and waist tabs. The suit has two open pockets set diagonally on the chest with two further open shin pockets. Unlike the orange boiler suit, there is no elastic at the rear of the waist. The life vest, pistol belt and holster are worn under the parachute harness and the knife, scabbard and clipboard are strapped to the legs. Note the stitching on the cuffs, the pistol belt, and the crimped edge to the Air Vest in Plate 13.3.

Scramble Crash Helmet
The white plastic Scramble crash helmet also formed the basic mould for all subsequent helmets of this type (see Plates 31.1, 53.1, 56.1 and 95.1). The visor is made from two pieces – a semi-circular golden strip with pivot pins, and a transparent green eyeshade. The black polyurethane face mask fits to either side of the helmet with a simple pin and hole arrangement, again a standard pattern for other, later pieces. The facemask is in turn attached to an orange polyurethane ribbed hose, which has a separate black nozzle and a diagonal stalk at the end. The orange stripe on the top of helmet ends with a circular blue and green winged insignia and the name 'ACTION MAN' in blue. A circular piece of foam was also glued into the crown of the helmet.

On First Issue pieces the badges were made from paper stickers, but this later issue piece features weaker coloured airbrushed stencilling.

Parachute Pack
The Parachute Pack, made of the standard green heavy weave material, was filled out on the equipment card with a folded corrugated cardboard insert. In the centre is the waist strap – adjusted by a large rectangular buckle, a design not used on any other Action Man piece. At the bottom are looped straps for the legs which attach to the bottom of the golden polyurethane cross-shaped quick-release buckle (see Plate 13.3), the buckle clipping on to the top straps with thick brass clips. A single popper fastens the top flap. All straps on this piece are double thickness and double sewn.

PARACHUTE PACK

Put Action Man's legs through here
CHEST STRAPS
QUICK RELEASE ASSEMBLY
LEG STRAPS

Insert Action Man's legs behind Quick Release Assembly, then forward through Leg Straps and pull up, as shown. Bring Chest Straps over the shoulder and fasten in front to the Quick Release Assembly. Last, buckle Waist Band over parachute assembly straps.

13. SCRAMBLE

13.1

14. SURVIVAL SET

QUARTERMASTER

- inflatable life raft
- oar
- rope and sea anchor
- flare gun
- knife and scabbard
- first aid kit

SPECIAL FEATURES

Life Raft
The yellow inflatable life raft, which is only big enough to take one survivor, is seen here beached with all the survival gear from the Set. Plate 14.1 shows the plastic wooden oar (similar to the Medic's splints and crutch) held in two of the raft's four loops, the silver plastic flare gun, the sea anchor and rope plus a small red First Aid box. The other main set, which included an identical life raft, was the Navy Sea Rescue Set; but this did not include the Air Vest. Note the Life Raft lettering and surrounding rectangle stencilling.

First Aid box
Made from two separate parts with a Hasbro ® inscription on the separate base, the First Aid box was issued with the two life raft sets and the separate Survival Set equipment card.

Air Vest
The Air Vest is made of two main pieces of orange PVC with a thin section of foam in between. The PVC is heat sealed and crimped around the complete edge and has a sub-divided front body section. On the lower right hand corner is stencilled lettering with a square surround. At the back are three straps – one at the top and in each bottom corner. These are fastened with a figure of eight ring linking through brass rings on each of the bottom straps.

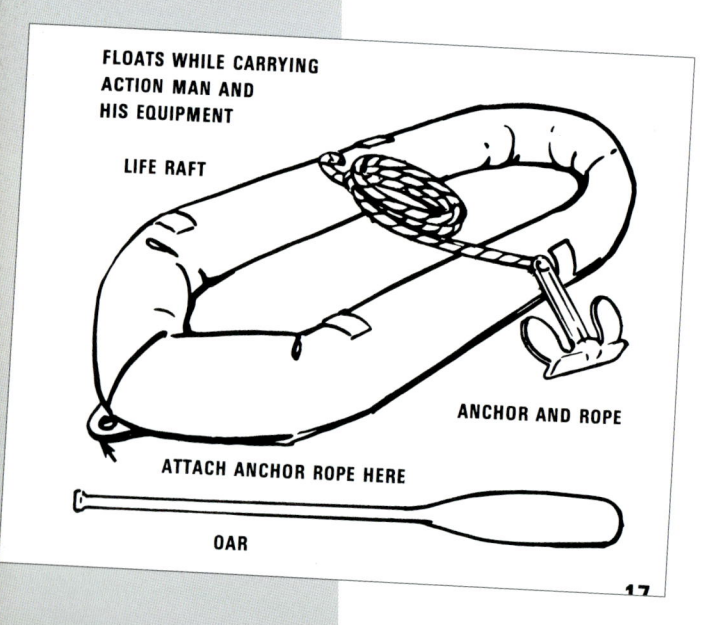

FLOATS WHILE CARRYING ACTION MAN AND HIS EQUIPMENT

LIFE RAFT

ANCHOR AND ROPE

ATTACH ANCHOR ROPE HERE

OAR

14.1

14. SURVIVAL SET

15. AIR POLICE

QUARTERMASTER

Separate Equipment Card:
- white A1 stencilled AP helmet
- grey field telephone, with case
- M1 carbine
- bayonet

Separate Equipment Card:
- field radio
- clipboard, pad and pencil
- binoculars
- map and case

Separate Equipment Card:
- jacket and tunic

The equipment, notably the white A1 helmet and grey field telephone case, is part of the range available on First Issue equipment cards. However the airforce blue uniform was not shown in any manual until the Quartermasters Stores uniform cards were introduced in the 1970's.

SPECIAL FEATURES

Uniform
The uniform comprises a single-breasted tunic with three poppers at the front. The neck is open and there are two square pleated and pointed flap breast pockets. Above the left pocket is a single tier medal ribbon. The hip pockets are square and covered by a rectangular flap. These lower pockets are sewn to the body of the jacket at the top and bottom edges only. There are also two plain epaulettes, but no separate cuffs. The back is a single piece of plain material with no vents and the tunic features ten circular silver buttons. The trousers are plain with a double sewn waist and two open square pockets. They are fastened at the rear by a single popper.

Accessories
The grey version of the field telephone is clearly shown in Plate 15.3, together with the white pistol belt and holster plus the white truncheon (also included in the Naval Dress Parade equipment card). Note the shape of the standard A1 helmet in this profile shot.

15. AIR POLICE

15.1

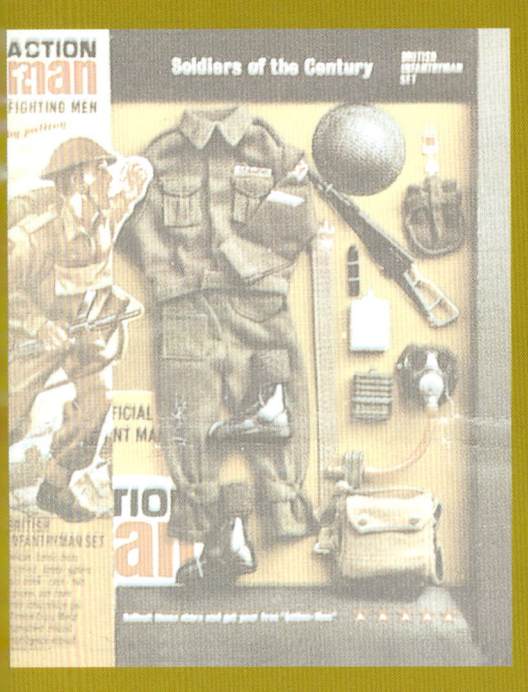

A dramatic extension of the Action Man range occurred when the six Soldiers of the Century sets were introduced during 1967/1968. Available in one main set or on two rectangular equipment cards, these were the first sets to move away from the core US forces' uniforms and equipment of the initial 1966 releases, though most were still based on the World War Two era. Production of these uniforms was not constant with the American Green Beret being withdrawn from the range as the first casualty. However the original German Stormtrooper, British Infantryman and French Resistance Fighter remained available in service for the longest initial period. A new and later addition was the French Foreign Legionnaire in the Soldiers of the World series. Each Soldiers of the Century Set came supplied with an Intelligence Manual providing details of the different uniforms, rank insignia, weapons from the countries included in the series, plus Morse Code sequences. The first type of manual had a black card cover and the Soldiers of the World versions had cream/pink paper covers.

48

RS OF NTURY

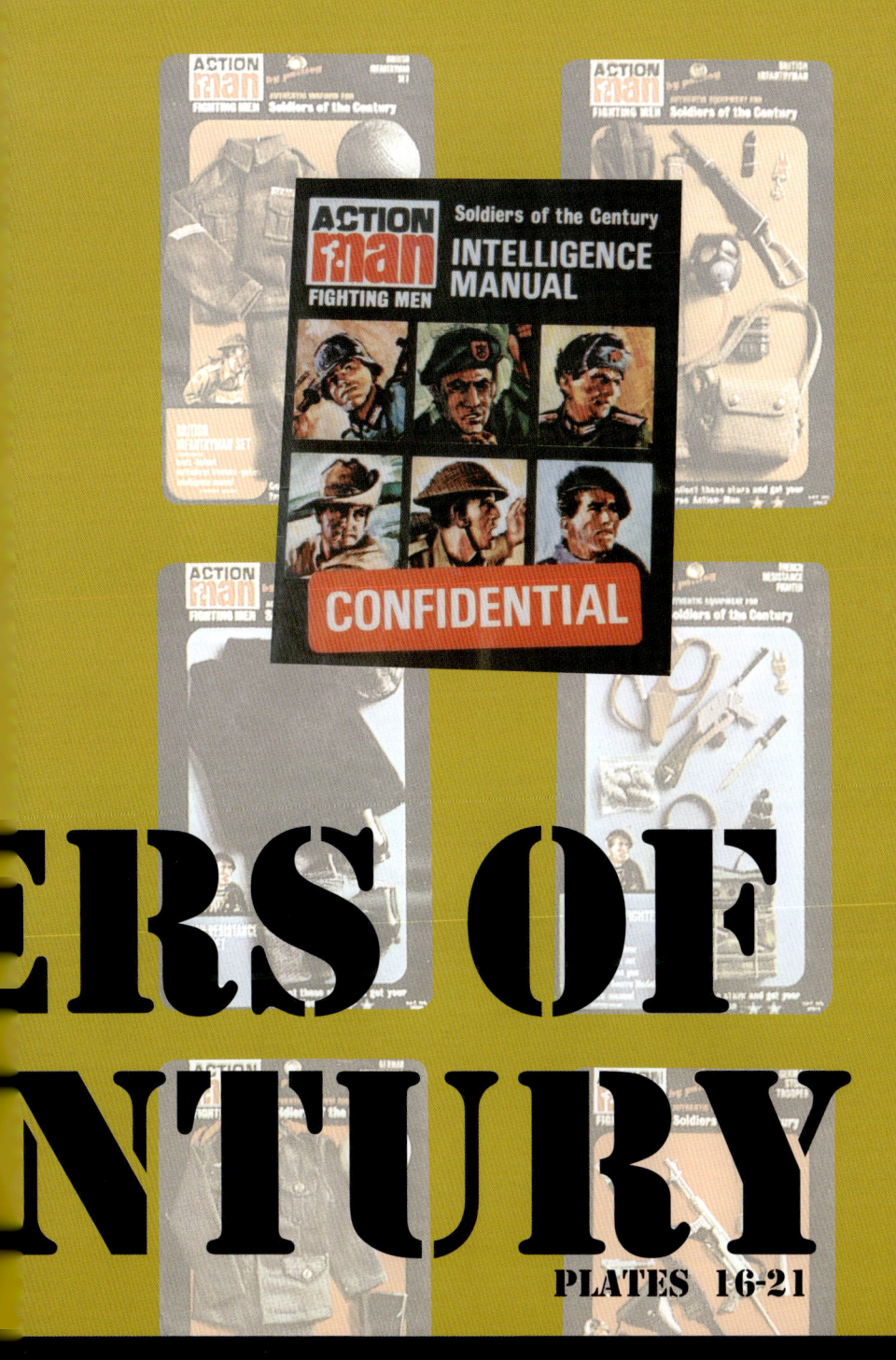

PLATES 16-21

16. GERMAN STORMTROOPER

QUARTERMASTER

- helmet
- tunic and trousers
- marching boots
- cartridge belt
- field pack
- grenades
- Luger pistol and holster
- 'Schmeisser' MP38/40 submachine gun
- Iron Cross

This set was based on a Blitzkrieg era combatant. The actual stormtrooper uniform went through a significant simplificatio as World War II progressed with the introduction of plain pocket ankle boots and gaiters instead of the more infamous jackboot (included in this set).

SPECIAL FEATURES

Helmet
Plate 16.1 shows the light grey plastic coalscuttle 1935 pattern *Stahlhelm* wi the red, white and black national colours on the outsize right shield badge. The corresponding left helmet shield badge is black with a white eagle and swastika device. The First Issue helmet badges were transfers whereas later issue versions used paper stickers. During the War the Germans phased out first the right tricolour badge in 1940 and then the left eagle badge in 1943. The red *Waffenfarbe* denotes that the wearer is part of an artillery unit. The Germans used different coloured piping on their uniforms to denote the diffe ent arms of service, examples being white for the infantry, pink for panzers o orange for cavalry units. The red collar patches are a basic rep resentation of the actual service badge; a better version was included in the late issue uniform shown on Plate 60.1. Clearly illustrated here is the eagle emblem over the right breast. This made of woven silver thread on a green ribbon strip and is glu onto the jacket.

Jacket and Trousers
The jacket and trousers are made of a heavy grey green materia The jacket represents a single breasted 1936 pattern service tunic with three poppers and buttons. There are two rounded and pleated breast pockets with pointed flaps, and two pointe flap hip pockets. All the pockets are fastened with a dark gree button, as are the epaulettes. At the rear of the jacket there is central back seam and vent, with darts in front and rear of the tunic providing shape. The trousers are fastened with one popp at the waist, and there are black four-cord elastic loops at eac ankle so that the leg of the uniform fits into the jackboot witho riding up.

Grenades
The two 1915 pattern 'potato masher' grenades can be tucke into either the wearer's belt or the top of the boot. The Actio Man grenades are made from two halves of silver plastic; wooden parts are painted a light sand or buff colour (later iss pieces had a darker or chocolate brown paint). The small cap on the base of the original weapon was unscrewed and the friction ignitor set by pulling two internal cords, before detonating the explosive charge in the large cylindrical head.

Boots
First Issue pieces are made of a shinier plastic. Unlike later versions, the moulded black polyurethane marching boots hav no numbers embossed on the soles.

16. GERMAN STORMTROOPER

16.1

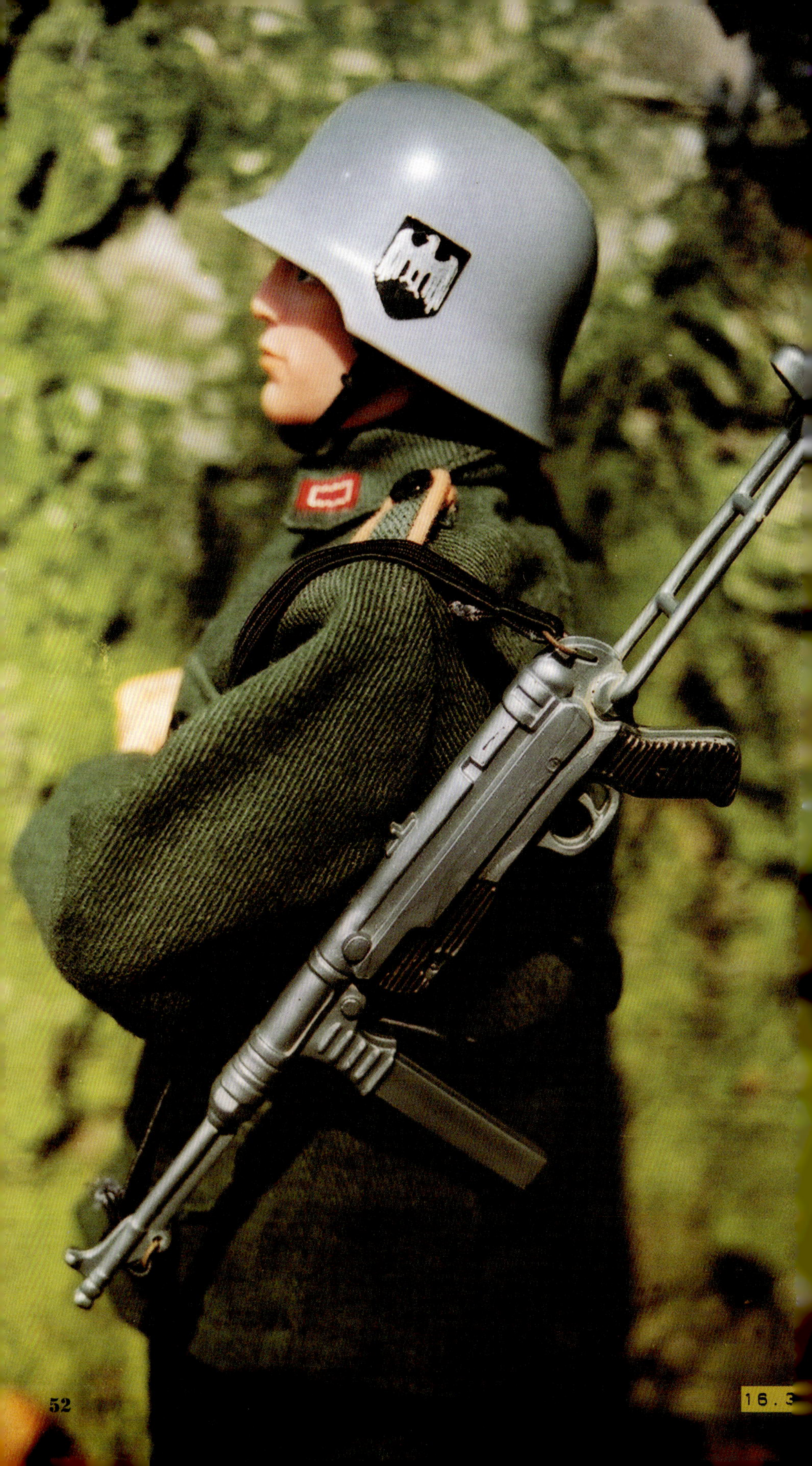

MP 38/40
Plate 16.3 is a fine study of the 9mm Machine Pistol 1938/1940. The MP38/40, is incorrectly called the Schmeisser, after the surname of the manager of the Erma factory where the weapons were manufactured. The Action Man piece is made from two components in silver plastic: the stock, which has two strengthening struts not on the original weapon, and the main body of the gun with its 32 round box magazine. The stock is glued on and cannot be folded underneath the gun's body. The black six-cord elastic strap is connected by brass rings at the rear of the gun and at the end of the barrel. Black paint on the grip and body's grooved section is the only other feature of this piece.

Also shown is a later orange *waffenfarbe* version of the tunic and a later issue helmet with sticker insignia. (Note also the diagonal weave of the uniform material and the missing helmet swastika).

Iron Cross and Belt
The Iron Cross in Plate 16.5 is shown in the First Class position (the Second Class medal was attached to a buttonhole on the main seam of the tunic). The medals for the Soldiers of the Century series are made from a metal base with one or two spikes allowing the decoration to be fixed to the jacket. To this was stuck a paper medal ribbon, in this instance a black and white stripe pattern. The embossing on the alloy cross and the circle above it can be clearly seen, as can the belt buckle with the oak leaf circle and eagle insignia.

Ammunition pouches and Belt
Regrettably the two sets of ammunition pouches shown are not for the MP38/40 weapon supplied with the Set but the bolt action Mauser rifle included in the later Afrika Korps Set and the last issue Stormtrooper. The Action Man pouches are subdivided into three sections which hold 2 five round clips of 7.92mm ammunition each. The pouches can be slid around the belt as required. The First Issue belt itself is made of stiff black PVC with a moulded 'pebbled' finish. It is connected to the buckle by two lugs on either side – the right is fixed with looped PVC on a heat sealed bond; the left side holds the clip which allows the belt to be fastened together.

Field Pack
Plate 16.4 provides some detail of the helmet's angled neck guard and the Tornister fur covered pack. The fur pack was mainly used for formal occasions such as drill or rallies. In combat, the looser assault pattern equipment – entrenching tool, gas mask, zeltbahn cape, mess tin, breadbag and waterbottle – was favoured in conjunction with 'Y' straps which connected to the stormtrooper's belt. The pack supplied with the Action Man Stormtrooper Set is made of a greener material than the tunic and trousers and is fastened by a single popper under the synthetic fur material flap. The straps of the pack are fixed by two buckles and a further two straps can be fastened to the wearer's belt with the D clips similar to those used for the Medic's bag.

NOT SHOWN – Luger pistol and holster (see Plates 81.1 and 82.2)

17. RUSSIAN INFANTRYMAN

QUARTERMASTER

- fur lined hat
- jacket and trousers
- marching boots
- belt
- binoculars and case
- anti tank grenades
- ammo box
- DP light machine gun
- bipod
- magazine
- Order of Lenin

SPECIAL FEATURES

Fur Hat
The fur *shapka-ushanka* hat has a red enamel star shaped badge and is made s that the earflaps can be tied under the wearer's chin with cotton cords. On First Issue examples the fur is thick and lighter grey in colour, whereas later issues are made from a cheaper material, thinner and darker. The base of the hat is made of a light grey material with cross stitching across the oval shaped crown.

Uniform
A single breasted *mundir* tunic was introduced in by the Russians in 1943. Plate 17.1 illustrates the reed green colour of the tunic and the jodhpur shaped M1935 *sharovari* trousers. The thick weave of the material can be seen, as can the row of four green buttons. The tunic has two darts on each breast and a separate skirt is sewn to the waist. It has a star collar and plain cuffs; the back features an overlapping vent with four buttons. Plate 17.3 provides some detail of the breast darts and tunic skirt and the red and gold Order of Lenin medal with its singl spike. The boots are of the same pattern as the Stormtrooper's.

Degtyarev DP
This was the main Russian light machine gun introduced into servic in 1933. The 7.62mm ammunition was housed in the 71 round dru on the top of the weapon. The Action Man piece comprises three parts: the drum with a series of circular holes and moulded ridges, the gold painted bipod and the main body of the gun itself – a sing silver plastic mould with a gold painted flash suppresser on the barrel, and a redbrown painted butt. There is no Hasbro inscription but there is a mould number, in this instance an 8, on the gun's bu

Ammunition Box
The ammo box is made from three components: the green plastic body with the three sets of horizontal stripes and a stencilled star the lid and the polyurethane light green handle which is inserted through two lugs on the lid (the box is not big enough to house t circular drum or magazine).

Belt and Binocular Case
The PVC brown belt is of a similar design to the Stormtrooper's. The hammer and sickle clasp insignia, with the buckle lug and clip, has heat seal marks which can be clearly seen in Plate 17.3. This piece was moulded with a textured finish and the First Issue examples are very thick and stiff. Slung across the infantryman's shoulder is the binocular case. The case is of the same PVC material as the field telephone cover from the Combat sets and features a strap on the lid, which fastens to the main body of the case with a gold polyurethane pin.

NOT SHOWN – anti tank grenades.
(see Plate 73.1 and 73.2)

This set is perhaps the most historically incongruous with pink shoulder board ribbons over plain epaulettes, and an indistinguishable pink ribbon collar rank badge with a line of gold thread horizontally through the middle. The Intelligence Manual only gives shoulder board details so it is not possible to discern a rank for this soldier.

17. RUSSIAN INFANTRYMAN

17.1

18. FRENCH RESISTANCE FIGHTER

QUARTERMASTER

- beret
- black sweater
- trousers
- ankle boots
- radio set
- Lebel pistol and shoulder holster
- 7.65mm submachine gun
- knife
- grenades
- Croix de Geurre

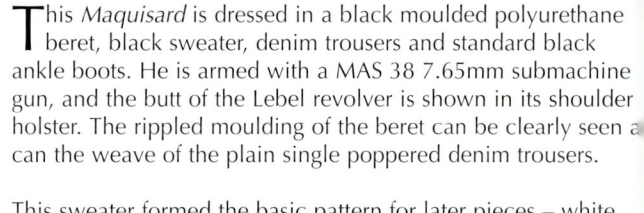

This *Maquisard* is dressed in a black moulded polyurethane beret, black sweater, denim trousers and standard black ankle boots. He is armed with a MAS 38 7.65mm submachine gun, and the butt of the Lebel revolver is shown in its shoulder holster. The rippled moulding of the beret can be clearly seen a can the weave of the plain single poppered denim trousers.

This sweater formed the basic pattern for later pieces – white and blue for explorers, and green for the mountaineer. Made from ribbed cotton material the sweater is made from six pieces main front and back, cuffs, waistband and neck. An 'Action Man' ribbon is sewn into a side seam.

SPECIAL FEATURES

Field Communication Set
The camouflaged Field Communication Set is common with the Green Beret Set. In Plate 18.1 it is in the open position, showing the four dials and two meters on the green printed paper lid insert together with the green plastic headphones. These have separate black plastic earpieces which are connecte to the black polyurethane Morse code unit by black coated wire. The body o the communication set itself is divided into two unequal sections to house th headphones and the Morse unit. Lid hinges are made from a pin heat riveted through the circular body and lid lugs.

MAS 38 submachine gun
Moulded from a single piece of silver plastic, the 7.65mm submachine gun h a painted black barrel and chocolate brown butt and grip handle. A Hasbro Hong Kong inscription is on the butt. A green six-cord elastic strap is fitted with a brass ring at the base of the barrel, and a pin and slot in the butt, simi to the arrangement on the M1 carbine shown in Plate 7.1. The original box magazine would hold 30 rounds.

Lebel Pistol and Shoulder Holster
This six round Lebel revolver was based on the 1892 8mm model which was also included in the Jungle Explorer and Royal Canadian Mounted Police Sets. The First Issue Action Man pieces are distinguished by their straight sided hexagonal barrels, later versions have rounded barrels. The rear view in Plate 18.2 shows the pin arrangement for the brown polyurethane shoulder holster. The holes and stitching on this single moulded piece can also be seen.

Knife
The knife is a First Issue example with a pointed blade. Later issue pieces, notably for the Afrika Korps Set, or the last Stormtrooper have blunted tips.

NOT SHOWN – Croix De Guerre medal.

18. FRENCH RESISTANCE FIGHTER

18.1

19. BRITISH INFANTRYMAN

QUARTERMASTER

- helmet
- battle dress tunic and trousers
- ammunition boots
- gaiters
- belt
- gasmask and bag
- canteen and cover
- Sten submachine gun
- Magazine
- Victoria Cross

SPECIAL FEATURES

Sten Gun
This Set was issued with a 9mm Mark II Sten gun (the weapon itself designed by **S**hepperd and **T**urpin at the Royal **En**field factory). This piece again features two support struts on the stock, which were not part of the original. The separate 32 round magazine fitted into a socket on the left side of the gun's body and here is clearly shown the black four-cord elastic strap fitted to the gun via the brass rings. There is a Hasbro ® Hong Kong inscription above the trigger box.

Gasmask and Bag
The green polyurethane small box respirator is shown in Plate 19.2 with clear circular plastic eye pieces (omitted in later versions). The green polyurethane facemask fastens with a green six-cord elastic strap riveted to each side of the mask and a plastic silver centre piece connects the orange ribbed hose to a two part filter at the base of the piece. The heavy weave sand coloured canvas gas mask bag shown in Plate 19.1 is in the 'alert' position, with the cord from the right going around the body of the wearer and then tied through a cord loop on the lower left side of the bag. Note the rivet type poppers on the bag flap.

Uniform
The battledress tunic has two square pleated and pointed flap breast pockets. It has separately stitched cuffs and two plain epaulettes. The waistband is double stitched around the bottom of the tunic in a similar fashion to the MP's 'Ike' jacket shown in Plate 4.3. The tunic has two back pleats and is fastened with four poppers (the trousers have two). The 1937 pattern battledress trousers are designed with separate ankle tabs. On the right hip is an open square pocket On the left thigh is a sewn outline of another rounded pocket; this has a separate pointed flap, with buff coloured lining, sewn in a closed position.

Insignia
The rank stripes and unit insignia are made from ribbon, machine embroidered, cut and then stuck onto appropriate positions on the sleeves of the battledress tunic. Plate 19.1 illustrates clearly the crossed swords unit badge and the two tier medal ribbon whilst Plate 19.3 shows the detail of the brass alloy Victoria Cross

Boots
The black ammunition boots are a distinct departure from other sets as the flexible plastic has five sets of eyelet holes and actual cotton laces. The boots are marked with moulded stitching on the heel and toecaps, plus a mould number, 1 to 4, a letter 'T' and a Hasbro Hong Kong inscription on the sole.

> The Mk II steel helmet was a development of the original version introduced by the British during World War One. The Mk II pattern of helmet remained in service until the advent of the new Mk III version in 1942.

Also included in the Set are green twenty-two cord elastic gaiters and a water bottle. The water bottle cover has an inner square pocket and a cross and loop set of straps with popper fastener which fits around a standard sand Combat pistol belt.

NOT SHOWN – cante

A Tommy with corporal's insignia was the first set to denote any distinguishable rank other than private. The uniform is made of a thick earth/green material with a discernible diagonal weave. Later issue sets are of either a far greener hue or made from thinner material with no weave pattern.

19. BRITISH INFANTRYMAN

19.1

20. AUSTRALIAN JUNGLE FIGHTER

QUARTERMASTER

- campaign hat
- jacket and shorts
- socks
- boots
- flamethrower
- jungle knife
- entrenching tool
- machete and sheath
- grenades
- Victoria Cross

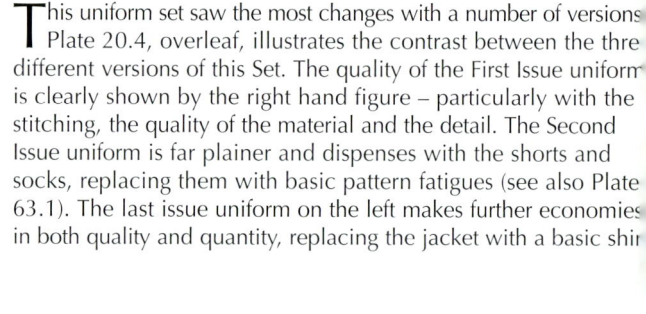

This uniform set saw the most changes with a number of versions Plate 20.4, overleaf, illustrates the contrast between the three different versions of this Set. The quality of the First Issue uniform is clearly shown by the right hand figure – particularly with the stitching, the quality of the material and the detail. The Second Issue uniform is far plainer and dispenses with the shorts and socks, replacing them with basic pattern fatigues (see also Plate 63.1). The last issue uniform on the left makes further economies in both quality and quantity, replacing the jacket with a basic shirt

SPECIAL FEATURES

Bush Hat
The polyurethane khaki coloured campaign, or bush, hat is fastened at one side with a brass rivet and has a cloth hatband. Three air holes were moulded to both sides of this piece. First Issue bush hats are made of a more rigid material than later versions.

Jacket, Shorts and Socks
The single breasted khaki jacket seen in Plate 20.1 has square pleated breast pockets with pointed flaps and sand coloured buttons and features double stitched cuffs and plain epaulettes. There are three sand coloured buttons and three poppers. The plain, square hip pockets are stitched only at the top with no buttons on the rectangular flap; on the First Issue version a thin buff material was used to line these pockets. The belt has a square brass buckle and fits through two belt loops at the side of the jacket. The dark blue unit insignia on the left arm has a red horizontal 'Z' device and is based on the same ribbon design as other insignia in this series.

Knee length shorts have a separate deep waistband which is poppered, with two further poppers fastening the shorts themselves. There is one square open pocket on the back of the shorts, to the wearer's right. The rear view in Plate 20.2 shows the central vent and the darts in the back of the jacket, together with the separate shoulder yoke and the single seam at the rear of the socks. These socks are made of a single piece of ribbed material which have a loop of elastic sewn into the inside hem. The boots are a brown version of the Action Sailor's ankle boots.

Machete and Flamethrower
The tan coloured PVC machete sheath is looped through the double sewn jacket belt. Tucked into the belt are two standard Action Man fragmentation grenades and on right hand side is the gold hilted jungle knife. The machete is made from single piece of silver moulded plastic with handle painted in chocolate brown and three indented circles moulded on each side of the handle. The camouflage flamethrower is based on the same pattern as the piece shown in Plate 7.1.

The buff coloured entrenching tool lying in the sand provided the basis for subsequent models – the green version in the Special Operations Kit and the black one in the SAS Demolition Set.

NOT SHOWN – Victoria Cross (see Plate 19.3)

20. AUSTRALIAN JUNGLE FIGHTER

20.1

20.5

20. AUSTRALIAN JUNGLE FIGHTER

21. AMERICAN GREEN BERET

QUARTERMASTER

- beret
- fatigue jacket and pants
- boots
- camouflage scarf
- pistol belt
- field communication set
- M-16
- Colt .45 and holster
- grenades
- Silver Star

Separate Equipment Card:
- Rifle Rack
- M-16
- M79 grenade launcher
- M1 rifle
- M1 carbine

The first new contemporary Action Man set, with a uniform from the Vietnam conflict. The Set included a Colt M16A1 rifle. This original of this weapon held a magazine of 30 5.56mm rounds and was first introduced into US Army service in 1963.

SPECIAL FEATURES

M-16
The Action Man piece is made of three black plastic components: the main body, stock and barrel, and then two separate barrel grips which are glued around it. In the top of the grip are ten air cooling holes, with a further six at the bottom. The grained pattern butt is painted dark brown and the green six-cord elastic strap is connected to the piece with brass rings. There is one lug the barrel's end, one at the base of the butt as shown here, and one on the handle. The Hasbro ® Hong Kong inscription is on the butt.

Jacket and Trousers
The green fatigue jacket is made of a fabric with a ditsinct diagonal weave an fastens with three poppers. It has two rounded and slanted breast pockets wit internally sewn central seams and two buttons on each rectangular flap. The two larger hip pockets are of similar design and have an inner lining of thin green material; they are fastened to the jacket at the top only. The separately stitched wide cuffs are plain with no poppers and there are plain epaulettes o the shoulders. The back of the tunic is plain with two individual waist tabs. The belt is the basic standard sand coloured Combat type. The trousers have two thigh pockets, with two vertical pleats and a rectangular flap with poppe

The high black jungle boots are based on the original Action Pilot pattern.

Beret and Camouflage Scarf
The silk jungle pattern camouflage scarf is based on the red MP's version. Th beret has a red and black arrow and oakleaf badge. It is made of polyurethan with the alloy badge stuck into the moulded shape at the front. Note the cur of its shape in Plate 21.4.

M79 Rifle and Rack
The M79 was only initially available with the Rifle Rack pictured here. The rack housed six weapons, in this case M16's. The Action Man M79 is made of brown plastic with silver and gold painted sections and a black four-cord elastic strap is connected with brass rings. There is a Hasbro Hong Kong ® inscription on the butt and the sight is moulded in the upright position.

The M79 40mm Grenade Launcher, or 'Blooper' gun, was a single shot breech loading weapon.

NOT SHOWN – Silver Star and camouflaged Field Communication Set (see Plate 18.1).

21. AMERICAN GREEN BERET

21.1

3D
ACTION
man
OFFICIAL
EQUIPMENT
MANUAL

OFFICIAL
EQUIPMENT
MANUAL
PALITOY REGD
ACTION
man
the movable fighting man

2ND WAVE

PLATES 22-33

There had been no new Action Man releases since the brand was first launched and collections of the First Issue equipment were accumulated. In 1967 a new series of mainstream equipment was introduced alongside the Soldiers of the Century series, and this chapter focuses on these new Soldier, Pilot and Action Man Sailor sets. Unlike the Soldiers of the Century series, all the uniforms and equipment shown here further the US forces theme with no other countries' uniforms being represented. Some of the pieces included here were not illustrated in any equipment manual of the period.

22. BAZOOKA

QUARTERMASTER

Separate Equipment Card:
. Bazooka
. two shells

Equipment Centre Card:
. pilot's overall

22.1

SPECIAL FEATURES

Bazooka
This weapon is based on the US 2.36" rocket launcher, which was first introduced into service in 1943. The Action Man piece is made of two 5" tubes, male and female, and a spring operated firing mechanism. It can fire the gold coloured polyurethane shell over 20 feet. Both tubes are camoufla with light green dapple shapes. A Hasbro ® Singapore inscription can be se between the shoulder rest and the trigger mechanism. Plate 22.2 illustrates one of the hollow shells.

22. BAZOOKA

Beret
An example of the blue polyurethane beret introduced with the new basic soldier figure. Based on the original Green Beret pattern, it has an eight pointed star and inverted crown badge.

Overalls
The grey/green one piece overall has an eagle badge on the left breast and is from a late issue Equipment Centre card. The pattern is based on the original Action Pilot piece from Plate 12.1.

23. MINE DETECTION SET

QUARTERMASTER

- electric mine detector with battery pack
- carrying case
- headset
- three mines

SPECIAL FEATURES

The silver plastic cylindrical battery case is carried in a First Issue heavy weave backpack and connects to a plastic gold coloured detector. The metal connection on the base of the detector head complete an electrical circuit when they touch some of the raised points on the mine, lighting up the bulb on the detector's battery case. The pole is moulded with a housing for both the black and white sticker dial and the red and white wires which are connected to the battery case. Note the adjustable straps for the carrying case.

The rear view in Plate 23.2 shows the battery pack and case in more detail. The belt is an integral part of the webbing and is made with the double width material, triple stitching patterns, buckles and D shaped hooks to First Issue Combat equipment standard.

Also included with this Set are the black headphones shown in Plate 23.1. The headphone earpieces are riveted to a semi-circular head clip.

NOT SHOWN – the circular metal mines (see Plate 64.1)

23.2

23. MINE DETECTION SET

23.1

24. LANDING SIGNAL OFFICER

QUARTERMASTER

- landing signal suit
- two signal paddles
- cloth helmet
- headphones
- binoculars
- clipboard, pad and pencil
- goggles
- flare gun

All the accessories, excluding the suit, were also available on a separate equipment card. No boots were issued with this Set

SPECIAL FEATURES

Signal Suit
The signal suit is based on a standard one piece overall modelled on the design from Plate 12.1. There are two types of reflective stripes stitched on to the buff material – thick magenta ones on the front of the arms, and two thinner vertical orange ones either side of the zip. The back of the suit is plain with no stripes.

Signal Paddles
The signal paddles are single moulded plastic pieces and have a Hasbro ® inscription on each buff painted handle. Wires from the handle connect to a solid plastic bat and a further wire protrudes along the top of the piece. Orange and magenta striped paper is glued around each bat.

Helmet
The helmet is made of bright yellow cotton with a popper-fastening chinstrap. Earpieces from the headphones fit into two cloth circles on the sides of the helmet and these hold them in place. The back of the helmet is square shaped and on the crown are two flaps, fastened by two poppers, which also help to keep the headphones in place. The goggles are identical to those issued with the Ski Patrol Set (see Plate 6.1)

NOT SHOWN – binoculars, clipboard, pad, pencil, and flare gun. (see Plates 10.1, 12.1, 14.1.)

24. LANDING SIGNAL OFFICER

24.1

25. CRASH CREW SET

QUARTERMASTER

- firefighter's jacket and trousers
- protective hood with visor
- boots
- gloves
- fire extinguisher
- crash belt
- axe
- strap cutter
- pliers
- flashlight

SPECIAL FEATURES

Protective Suit
This was the last of the Action Pilot series. The protective hood is large enough to cover the wearer's shoulders. Its curved green plastic visor is fixed to the silver coated material by brass rivets in each corner and helps to hold the hood in place. The plain patterned jacket and trousers are made of the same silver coated material. The jacket is plain, fastening with two poppers, whilst the trousers feature rectangular outline-stitched knee patches. Note the double stitching on the hood, the hem of the jacket, and the hood rivets.

Gloves are based on the familiar mitt pattern, with a separate thumb; for this piece the backs are made of silver coated material with palms of plain black cotton material. The silver plastic boots were moulded on the original ski boot pattern.

Fire Extinguisher
The large fire extinguisher comprises four components. A red plastic base has a gold valve at the top which is connected to the black PVC tube and the funnel. The funnel can be clipped to the base as shown.

Belt Accessories
The black PVC belt has pouches at the back which hold the pliers, strap cutter and red angle-headed torch. To the right is a slot for the axe. The PVC of the belt and pouches is heat sealed with crimped edging.

The golden polyurethane pliers are riveted together with a pin and will open and shut. Note the serrated edge to the silver painted head of the red plastic axe in Plate 25.3.

> This angle-headed torch forms the basic pattern for later green versions included in both the Colditz Set and the Special Operations Kit.

25. CRASH CREW SET

26. COMMANDER

QUARTERMASTER

- beret
- jacket and trousers
- black boots
- pistol belt
- Colt .45
- holster

The uniform for this Set is based on the basic Action Soldier fatigues (see Plate 1.1) but with high combat boots in black rather than brown. This Set extended the range of Green Beret pattern berets with a new black version.

SPECIAL FEATURES

Insignia
The crest badge is red with a black crown device above an eight pointed star. First Issue versions featured paper sticker unit badges for each arm of the jacket: a curved black title badge with white lettering 'AM COMMANDER', and underneath a red, white and blue chequered square with crowns on the white squares. Over the left breast is a paper sticker two tier medal ribbon. T. metal captain's rank bars are based on the US insignia, with spikes in each corner which are crimped onto the uniform astride the shoulder seam.

Pistol and Holster
The pistol belt is the sand coloured Combat version, although some Equipme Manual pictures show a green piece first introduced in the Jungle Fighter equipment card together with a canteen and cover, jungle knife, and machete Plate 26.2 provides some detail of the standard Colt M1911 A1 .45 automatic pistol. Note the adjustable polyurethane belt loop.

26. COMMANDER

27. INFANTRY SUPPORT WEAPONS

QUARTERMASTER

- flak jacket
- M60 machine gun
- Ammunition belt
- 81mm mortar
- baseplate
- bipod
- three mortar shells

Another contemporary set, this also includes a flak jacket, or bullet proof vest. These were in regular service with the US forces in Vietnam.

SPECIAL FEATURES

M60 Machine Gun
This Action Man piece is moulded from a single piece of steel grey plastic. The butt and grip are painted black with the handle and front sight spray painted gold. The silver polyurethane ammunition belt fits through a slot just behind the sight. Hasbro ® Hongkong is inscribed just above the pistol grip. The bipod is fitted at the end of the barrel and has three components – the tw adjustable legs, which can be folded back along the barrel, and the barrel sleeve, which fits around the sight.

The M60 general purpose machine gun replaced the earlier Brownings as the standard US weapon of its type. A derivative of the German MG42 this 7.62mm weapon was introduced into US service in 1960 and had a rate of fire of 550 rounds per minute.

Flak Jacket
The Action Man flak jacket has three main fabric parts: back, front a the lower front abdominal skirt. Made of the same weight material a the Combat sleeping bag, extra body is provided by a foam insert between the layers of material. Edged with a separate single stitched border, the vest fastens with two poppers on each side. The jacket is pulled on over the wearer's head.

The close up shot in Plate 27.2 shows two sets of four silver polyurethan bullets sewn to both sides of the chest through four pre-cast holes. Above them are sewn two brass rings connected to two standard fragmentation grenades. At the shoulders are two boards covered in light green fabric with a central white ribbon.

81mm Mortar
The 81mm mortar has a spring operated firing mechanism in the tube, which can lob a 'bomb' over 20 feet. The ribbed green plastic barrel is connected to a separate elevating rod, which swivels with the elevation of the weapon. A Hasbro ® Hong Kong inscription is moulded onto the smooth plastic section underneath the gold painted recoil device. Connected to this is the bipod and a thin chain with brass rings links one leg to the elevation pin. By inserting this pin in one of ten holes in the elevating rod, the range and trajectory of the mortar bombs can be varied. The circular black plastic baseplate is cast with a central gold painted slot for the base of the mortar tube and there is further gold painted casting on the outer rim. The underside of the baseplate has a Hasbro ® Hongkong inscription.

The figure in Plate 27.2 holds one of the Set's three silver plastic mortar bombs – each with four fins at the tail. Both heavy weapons from this Set were available on separate equipment cards, but the bullet proof vest was not.

27.2

27.

27.

78

27. INFANTRY SUPPORT WEAPONS

27.1

28. ARMOURED CAR COMMANDER

QUARTERMASTER

- commander jacket
- helmet
- pistol belt
- Colt .45
- holster
- Browning .30 calibre machine gun
- ammo box
- radio and tripod

The first 'hard' green polyurethane vehicles were introduced this time and this Commander's Set was released to compliment them.

SPECIAL FEATURES

Jacket
The buff coloured PVC zippered jacket has fur trim on collar and cuffs. This is an intricate garment with two slash pocket flaps at the waist and a collar strap. The rear view in Plate 28.2 illustrates the large central pleat at the back of the jacket, the separately sewn bottom waist section and the sand-coloured, buttoned epaulettes.

Helmet
The helmet was a new design with moveable visor and black polyurethane mike pinned to the right side. A black four-cord elastic strap with no buckle, bear insignia paper sticker and an internal circular foam cushion complete the piece which was modelled on an original World War Two fibre helmet pattern issued to U.S. tank crews.

NOT SHOWN
A standard Colt, holster and sand coloured pistol belt were also included in the Set.

Radio and tripod, machine gun and ammo box (see Plates 9.4 and 100.1.)

28.2

80

28. ARMOURED CAR COMMANDER

29. SABOTAGE

QUARTERMASTER

- inflatable raft
- oar
- rope and sea anchor
- flare gun
- signal light
- radio set and headphones
- gas mask
- M3 submachine gun
- knitted cap
- binoculars
- dynamite
- detonator

The last in the line of the large Combat sets, Plate 29.1 shows all the equipment in this set. The knitted woollen cap can also be seen, together with the gas mask which has only the larger of the two original filter boxes at the end of its ribbed ho Shown here is the grey detonator and dark green radio based o the same pattern as the Field Communications Set from the Soldiers of the Century series (see Plate 18.1). The standard binoculars are moulded in red plastic in this set but the flare gu signal lamp and dynamite are of similar patterns to earlier sets.

SPECIAL FEATURES

Inflatable Raft
The inflatable raft is of the same pattern as the Survival version, but made in black PVC with no markings. The paddle is moulded in black plastic and th tip and handle are painted yellow.

M3 Submachine Gun
A new piece was the .45 calibre M3 'greasegun', an American copy of the successful German sub-machine guns used during World War Tw This weapon was introduced in 1942 and held 30 rounds in its ventral box magazine. The Action Man piece is moulded with th stock in the folded position. It is made of silver plastic, largely sp painted gold, with a black four-cord elastic strap. There is a Has ® inscription on the base of the body.

Detonator
This device has a moveable plunger and black polyurethane carrying strap. The detail on the later issue polyurethane version the cap is shown in Plate 29.2.

29.2

29.3

82

29. SABOTAGE

29.1

30. COMBAT ENGINEER

QUARTERMASTER

Separate Equipment Cards:
- theodolite
- jackhammer
- hardhat
- gloves
- pick
- shovel

Based on a series of rectangular equipment cards rather than one large boxed set. All six pieces in the series are illustrated

SPECIAL FEATURES

Theodolite
The theodolyte is a complex piece. It has three red and white striped legs and a central red mounting. This provides a bed for the black top mount, with its Hasbro ® inscription, which in turn houses a standard size compass and the moveable wheel and sight. Suspended from the red mounting is the gold spray painted bob weight. A close up of the theodolyte top mount and the tripod leg rivets is shown in Plate 30.2.

Jackhammer, Hardhat and Gloves
The jackhammer is another complicated and rare piece. The top houses an inner spring which allows the bottom tip to move up and down within its circular sleeve. The piece is made from grey plastic, which is largely spray painted gold except for the collar at the base. There are two moulded screw sections on each side, painted black, and separate rods which connect the base collar to the handles at the top of the piece, where there is a Hasbro ® inscription.

The orange plastic hardhat has six points at the top of the rim, and three prominent ridges on the crown; one of two air holes in the rim can be seen here. There is a Hasbro Hong Kong inscription on the inside of the crown. The grey gloves are based on the same pattern as the Ski Patrol pieces. Note the heavy weave of the material and the elasticated wrists.

Pick and Shovel
On the ground in Plate 30.1 are the single moulded wood plastic pick and shovel pieces. Hasbro ® Hong Kong inscriptions are moulded on the back of the curved shovel head, together with a mould number, and on the bottom of the pick handle.

> The Action Man logo stamped on the metal dog tag is a simplified version, with no bullet holes on the lettering.

84

30. COMBAT ENGINEER

31. RED DEVIL PARACHUTIST

QUARTERMASTER

- working parachute and pack
- jumpsuit
- crash helmet
- goggles
- boots
- reserve parachute pack

One of the most colourful sets depicting a member of this elite display team drawn from members of the Parachute Regiment.

SPECIAL FEATURES

Jump Suit
The red jump suit is based on the standard one piece suit pattern. On the left breast is an adhesive fabric badge with silver winged emblem on a black background.

Helmet. Goggles and Boots
The helmet, goggles and jump boots are based on the same First Issue pattern as previous sets. The white helmet has a black rim and simple black polyurethane chinstrap with 'Action Man Red Devil' stencilled in red on the front

Parachute
This early version of the parachute is made up of red, white and blue cotton quarter panels, later versions included a plain orange nylon parachute. The reserve parachute pack is filled with foam and glued together under the square front section. The pack fastens around the waist, and there are two vertical straps which fix onto the main chute's harness with D rings. The main Parachute Pack's harness is cut to the same pattern as the original Scramble version.

Plate 31.1 shows the rich green coloured cords that connected the parachute to the deep green polyurethane moulded backpack. There are six cords in total, bunched into two groups of three and knotted at each side of the pack at the top.

Plate 31.2 replicates an original Hasbro publicity shot

31.2

86

31. RED DEVIL PARACHUTIST

31.1

32. BREECHES BUOY RESCUE SET

QUARTERMASTER

Breeches Buoy
- oilskin trousers and jacket with hood
- breeches buoy and pulley
- flare gun
- signal light

RNLI Sea Rescue Set
- oilskin trousers and jacket with hood
- boots
- air vest
- breeches buoy and pulley

SPECIAL FEATURES

Oilskin Jacket and Trousers
Made of yellow PVC the oilskin jacket and trousers are based on the original Ski Patrol patterns with similar popper arrangements, elasticated ankles and wrists, and draw cords at the hood, waist of the trousers and at the base of the jacket. The oilskins are fairly transparent and have no pockets or separate badges. The word NAVY is stencilled in black on the left breast. The first issue knitted cap seen in Plate 32.2 is from the Sabotage Set.

Breeches Buoy
The Breeches Buoy harness is made of heavy orange weave material sewn around a circular white plastic rim and is cut with a generous waist seat and two leg holes. The harness connects to the pulley by four moulded white polyurethane 'ropes' that in turn are joined by rings to the black plastic pulley block. Inside the pulley block are two brass coloured plastic wheels which allow the breeches buoy to be pulled along the rope connecting the stricken craft to the rescue ship. A Hasbro ® Hong Kong inscription appears on the pulley block. No boots or ropes were provided with this Set.

Lifebelt
The white plastic NAVY lifebelt was issued on a separate Equipment Card.

RNLI Air Vest
Illustrated is the later RNLI version air vest with stencilled RNLI initials (Royal National Lifeboat Institution). Later versions of the oilskin jacket also have these initials.

NOT SHOWN
Signal lamp, (see Plate 9.2)

88

32. BREECHES BUOY RESCUE

32.1

33. ROYAL CANADIAN MOUNTED POLICE

QUARTERMASTER

- campaign hat
- tunic
- trousers
- boots
- Sam Browne belt
- pistol and holster

By collecting 18 Action Man Equipment stars you could send off for this Mountie set which was not available in the shops. The uniform comprises the campaign hat, the scarlet tunic, brown PVC Sam Browne belt, pistol and holster, navy blue jodhpur pattern trousers with yellow seam stripes and black boots moulded on the German/Russian Soldiers of The Century pieces.

SPECIAL FEATURES

Campaign Hat
The cream coloured plastic campaign hat has a four-dented 'Montana' crown. The hatband and buckle are similar to the PVC strap used on the field telephone cover from the Command Post Cape Set.

Tunic and Trousers
The scarlet tunic is of a heavy weave material with two square and pleated breast pockets and two plain square hip pockets.
All four pockets have scalloped flaps, but only the breast ones are fastened with gold plastic buttons. There are a further four buttons on the front seam of the jacket and two on each of the blue textured fabric epaulettes. Similar material adorns the edges of the stand collar, and these pointed blue flashes are fastened by a brass coloured metal crown and oakleaf badge; a two tier medal ribbon is sewn above the left breast pocket. There is a central seam at the back of the tunic and two black four-cord elastic belt loops on each side of the waist. Cuffs are plain, with three popper fasteners.

The trousers have one popper at the waist and a yellow co stripe sewn into the main leg seams.

Belt, Pistol and Holster
The Sam Browne belt has crimped edging and heat sealed standard hook clips, with two eyelets on the right for the shoulder strap hooks. The holster is made of the same material and cut in the First Issue standard pattern but with no eyelet or thigh strap. The pistol is of the same pattern a the Lebel included in the French Resistance Fighter Set but painted silver with a gloss brown painted grip. A hole is drilled into the grip to allow the neck cord to be threaded through it as shown in Plate 33.1.

33. ROYAL CANADIAN MOUNTED POLICE

33.1

35004 Base Camp

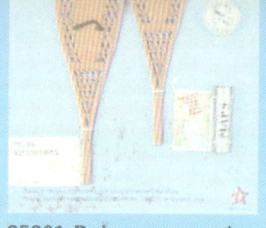

35201 Polar accessories

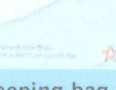

Sleeping bag

34813

SPORT
EXPL

Tent, flag, working stormlamp (battery not included), primus stove, mug, knife, fork, spoon, me... leaflet.

Polar accessories
Snow shoes, hat, compa... ster and...

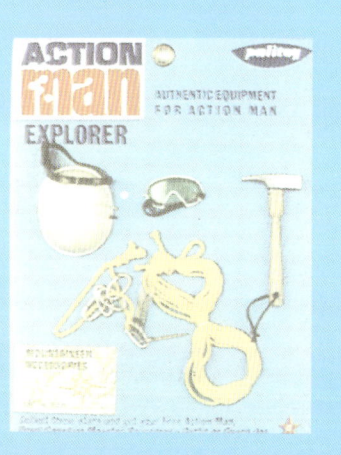

34816

SMEN
& RERS

34814 Everton   34815 West Ham United   34819 Newcastle United.

Football Club outfits all contain a tracksuit top with the club name printed across the back, socks, boots, ball, club history leaflet and club lapel badge for you to wear.

PLATES 34–42

The early 1970's saw a gradual introduction of civilians sets to the Action Man range. Four main sports sets were introduced, and initially there were three featured adventurers. The latter had a set of large accessories such as the riverboat, sledge, and base camp plus several equipment cards, which also enhanced the range. The advent of these sets marked the end of the First Issue equipment for the Combat Soldier, Action Sailor and Action Pilot whose main sets were all withdrawn by 1972. Some of the equipment was still available though in the Quartermasters Stores uniform and equipment cards, but the original woodgrain and red backed cards had gone.

34820 Celtic.   34817 Leeds United.   34818 Arsenal.

34. OLYMPIC CHAMPION

SPECIAL FEATURES

Singlet
The singlet is made of a white ribbed acrylic material with cotton arm and shoulder straps. The neckline of the singlet is low, as shown. Armholes and neckline are bound, with the binding of the neckline continued to form stra

The First Issue singlet is plain with no flag on the chest, as shown in Plate 3 Later issues have a Union Jack at the centre of the chest as in Plate 34.2.

Shorts and Shoes
The blue shorts have an elasticated waist with a double seam running dow the outside of each leg. The white polyurethane running shoes are made fr a single mould and have three diagonal yellow stripes painted on each sid Soles are inscribed Made in Hongkong.

Shot and Discus
The competitor in Plate 34.2 is holding the discus, which is moulded from a single piece of 'wood' colour plastic, with a spray painted silver rim. The Hasbro Hongkong inscription on the side can just be made out in this Plate.

The shot, seen in Plate 34.3, is moulded in silver grey plastic with the inscription 'Made in Hongkong' on the side.

Tracksuit
Plate 34.4 shows the First Issue orange tracksuit and th gold medal. The two piece tracksuit is elasticated at wa cuffs and ankles. The top is fastened with a zip but this fixed at the waist so the top must be pulled over the he of the figure. The medal is made from gold coloured p and has a laurel leaf pattern on the front and a Made i Hongkong inscription on the back. The plain blue ribb sewn with a single hem. Later issues of this Set use a d ent style of tracksuit made of a silky light blue material with red and white striped waist and cuff elastic.

NOT SHOWN – javelin, and special display stand.

QUARTERMASTER
- Track suit
- Singlet
- Shorts
- Running shoes
- Javelin
- Discuss
- Shot
- Medal
- Olympic torch
- Special display stand

34. OLYMPIC CHAMPION

34.1

35. CRICKETER

QUARTERMASTER

- cap
- white trousers
- white shirt
- sweater
- socks
- boots
- stumps
- bails
- bat
- ball
- display stand with artificial grass

SPECIAL FEATURES

Peaked Cap
The blue polyurethane peaked cap has a moulded indentation on the crest for the standard type of 'sports' badge, as shown in Plate 35.1. This edged badge, with laurel leaf design, was also used on the subsequent blue Equipment Care tracksuit and the footballer cards. 'Made in Hongkong' is inscribed on the bottom of the peak.

Sweater, Shirt and Trousers
The shirt is fastened with three crimped poppers, each with white enamel butt heads. There are similar poppers on each cuff but there are no pockets. The back and pointed collar are also plain. The trousers are made of heavier twill than the shirt and are fastened by a single white enamelled button popper. The raised creases on the edge of the trouser legs can be seen in Plate 35.2. The knitted sweater can be seen lying on the ground behind the stumps; it has a single blue band at the waist and around the V-neckline.

Boots
The seven eyelet white cricket boots were a common pattern with the Footballer Set, having four studs on the sole and two on the heel. There is a Made in Hongkong inscription on the bottom of each sole.

Bat, Stumps and Ball
The bat, stumps and bails are moulded from 'wood' colour plastic. All fit into the special display stand, which is painted with a crease line. The bat features a black PVC grip glued to the handle; there is a 'V' join moulded into the base on each side of the handle and a Made in Hongkong inscription on the bevelled side of the bat. The moulded stumps have pointed ends and a cradle for the bails.

Pads
The pads are made of a single white piece of moulded polyurethane. Plate 35.2 provides some detail of the knobbly straps which are fixed to the inner edge of each pad, and the three sets of buckles. An inverted Made in Hongkong inscription can be found on each pad.

NOT SHOWN – socks, bails, ball and special display stand which was painted.

35.2

35. CRICKETER

35.1

36. FOOTBALLER

QUARTERMASTER

- shirt
- shorts
- socks
- boots
- football
- display stand with artificial grass

Plus Different Club Sets For:
- Arsenal
- Celtic
- Chelsea
- Everton
- Leeds United
- Liverpool
- Manchester United
- Newcastle United
- Rangers
- West Ham United
- World Cup

Different Plain Coloured Equipment Cards:
- blue, blue stripes, green, red, white (one with black and one with white shorts), and a plain blue tracksuit.

The First Issue set, with plain red shirt, white shorts and red socks, is seen in Plate 36.1. It spawned a whole sub-series of ten English and Scottish First Division teams and then a further series of standard team colours on equipment cards.

The first series of football sets included a traditional panelled style of ball. The later 1970 English World Cup Footballer Set was the first to include the continental design of ball shown here (this example is not an original Action Man piece however, but supplied by the match sponsor – Barbie.)

SPECIAL FEATURES

Football Kit
The zipped tracksuit top is made of cotton, unlike the Olympic Champion's piece, and has a club badge on the left breast. The waist and cuffs are elasticated. In these Plates the player wears an example of a Manchester United player's tracksuit. The rear view in Plate 36.2 shows the name of the club.

The ribbed cotton socks do not have elasticated tops or hems. The single seam of the sock was sewn inside; the seam stitching then stops below the top and reversed so that when the top is turned over the seams are inside. Plate 36.2 shows some detail of these seams.

The white shorts are of a similar pattern to the shorts of the Olympic Champion. The shirt is made from the same material as the socks, with a single white enamel crimped button popper at the back of the neck.

36.2

36. FOOTBALLER

36.1

37. JUDO

QUARTERMASTER
- judogi
- grading belts

SPECIAL FEATURES

Judogi
The Equipment Centre version of this Set is illustrated here. Included are a p...
of simple white trousers and a Judogi jacket, plus three coloured grading bel...
– blue, brown and black. There are no poppers on the jacket and only one o...
the trousers. Note the plain cuffs and simple hem on the jacket, as seen in
Plate 37.2.

The First Issue version is made of a thicker, cream-coloured material with
reinforced knee sections and includes a wider range of coloured grading bel...

37.2

37. JUDO

37.1

38. JUNGLE EXPLORER

QUARTERMASTER
- bush hat
- tropical jacket and trousers
- bandana
- boots
- belt
- pistol and holster
- rifle
- machete and sheath
- jungle knife small pack and hypodermic darts

Rivercraft Set:
- canoe/raft
- working outboard motor
- two paddles
- two supply boxes
- rope

Jungle Accessories:
- rifle with telescopic sights
- jungle knife
- pith helmet
- water bottle and cover

SPECIAL FEATURES

Jungle Explorer Set
The Lincoln green open collar tropical jacket features two square, pleated breast pockets with pointed flaps. The large square hip pockets are plain, with a rectangular flap; the sleeves and epaulettes are also plain. There are two belt loops at either side of the waist. Fastened by two poppers, there are no buttons at all on this piece. A rear view in Plate 38.2 shows the separate shoulder yoke, central inverted pleat, waist darts and bottom vent. The cream trousers have two poppers, with four belt loops sewn to the waistband above the leg darts.

The belt has a square brass buckle and is made of brown leatherette with a black mottled finish. Attached is the machete and sheath – based on the same pattern as the Australian Jungle Fighter's piece except that the sheath is in dark brown and the handle of the machete is black.

Also shown in Plate 38.4 is the chocolate coloured holster for the pistol which is of the same pattern as the Lebel from the French Resistance Fighter Set. Strapped around the left leg is a knife and sheath similar to those included in the Frogman's Set.

The bush hat is made of double thickness cream coloured cotton and has a printed skin fabric hatband. The orange bandana is a simple double folded material tie, with a small triangular piece fitted into the stitching. High black boots the same as those supplied with the original Action Pilot (See Plate 12.1).

Jungle Accessories
The M1 pattern rifle is similar to the First Issue Combat pieces. The telescopic rifle from the accessories set in Plate 38.1. is moulded from a single piece of darker chocolate brown plastic with a separately painted buff fore grip and black metal work. The strap is made of black six-cord elastic and both barrel and scope are painted gold. Over the left shoulder in Plate 38.2 is the small pack, again based on an earlier piece, in this case the Unit One bag from the Medic Set (see Plate 5.1). Attached to the flap is a small row of bullets described as 'hypodermic darts' in the Equipment Manual. Note the Hasbro ® inscription.

Also shown in Plate 38.3 are the polyurethane pith helmet, the small pack, the Polar Explorer's rucksack and a green polyurethane jerry can from a late issue Equipment Centre card.

38. JUNGLE EXPLORER

38.1

38.4

Rivercraft Set
The canoe format of the Rivercraft is shown in Plate 38.4; two sections fasten together end to end with plastic U shaped clips. This allows a variation in which the two sections can be clipped side to side to form a raft. Also included in the Set are an outboard motor, two black paddles, two rectangular supply boxes and some yellow rope. The turquoise top section of the outboard motor lifts off to reveal a battery housing that drives the three bladed propeller. The outboard is fixed to the boat by a white clip; in the down position, this clip pushes up the connection in the battery housing to complete the circuit. Note the bulletless Action Man logo on the main body of the motor.

38. JUNGLE EXPLORER

Supply Boxes
Measuring 2.75" x 1.75" x 1.5", these boxes have two ridges running around all four sides and a white box number stuck to one side. The handles are of unequal length – one flat and the other full, requiring a rectangular cut in one end of the lid. The words 'Jungle' and 'Expedition' are engraved on two of the lid sections and then painted in red. A turquoise and black Action Man logo sticker is positioned on the third section.

The supply box lids can be clearly seen in Plate 38.3, an internal shot of the Riverboat.

39. MOUNTAINEER

QUARTERMASTER
- anorak
- jersey
- knee breeches
- socks
- boots
- rucksack
- ice hammer
- ice axe
- crampons
- pitons
- karibiners
- rope
- suckers

Separate Equipment Cards:
- helmet
- goggles
- ice axe
- pitons
- karibiners
- rope
- anorak
- high altitude equipment

Base Camp:
- tent
- flag
- storm lamp
- primus stove
- mug
- knife, fork and spoon
- mess tins
- billy can
- entrenching tool

Base Camp Accessories:
- radio transmitter
- storm lamp
- map and case

SPECIAL FEATURES

Anorak and Trousers
The vivid orange cotton anorak, with its chest pocket and plain rectangular flap, is shown in Plate 39.1. A machine embroidered Union Jack badge is sew to this front pocket. The cuffs are elasticated and there is a central flap at the back of the anorak which is connected to the front by a silver button popper. Draw cords are fitted to both waist and hood. The Mountaineer wears a pair brown corduroy knee breeches, which are fastened by a waist popper. Knee straps at the end of each leg are also fastened by poppers. Tied around the waist are a set of six grey polyurethane pitons, and four metal karibiners.

The figure in Plate 39.5 is wearing a light green anorak, from a later issue Equipment Centre card. Note the heavier draw cords at the waist.

Boots and Socks
Here the nylon socks are brown. First Issue versions were lime green – a similar colour to the sweater, which is cut to the same pattern as the black sweater introduced in the French Resistance Fighter Set. The brown polyurethane boots are of the same pattern as the black boots issued in the British Infantryman Set (See Plate 19.3). Fitted to these are silver polyurethane crampons, designed to fit over the boot and be fastened in place with small elastic bands.

Climbing Helmet and Hammer
The orange climbing helmet was not part of the main Mountaineer Set but w available on a separate accessory card; First Issue versions are white. A black polyurethane chinstrap is connected to the crown by a pin on each side of th helmet rim. In the right hand is held an ice hammer – a wood plastic handle with a silver painted head. Through the handle is threaded a thick loop of black single cord elastic. Note the yellow climbing rope held in the left hand

Rucksack
A 2.75" x 2" cotton and black leatherette rucksack can be seen in Plate 39.2. The main sack is made from blue cotton with a drawstring at the top. The carrying straps are black double-folded leatherette with standard buckles. Two straps and brass buckles hold the sack's flap in place. The base is of leatherette and there are two blue cotton waist ties, plus a loop for the ice pick, at the top of this leatherette section.

Base Camp Tent
The tent from the Base Camp Set is a complex piece which comes complete with nine tent wires and six black polyurethane corner connectors, enabling it to be put up anywhere. The resulting frame is made up of two triangles at each end, plus three connecting rods – the corners of the tent fabric are then attached to this structure. The fabric is tensioned with fo guy ropes fixed to loops and in turn hooked to the bottom wires at each end the tent. Unlike the Combat Pup Tent, there are no poles or pegs and the ten comes complete with a sewn in ground sheet. However only one end of the tent can be opened. The ground sheet is lime green as shown in Plate 39.3. Note the Primus stove, billy can and mug.

39. MOUNTAINEER

39.1

39.4

39.5

The end section illustrated in Plate 39.4 shows the guy rope hooks, tent ties and a complete end wire triangle. Also included in this Plate is the quilted, stitched sky blue polar sleeping bag, crampons and a pair of tan coloured Explorer's ankle boots. In the background can be seen the Union Jack flag which is of the same design and dimensions as the flag in the Medic Set (see Plate 5.3).

Primus Stove, Billy Can and Mug
The Primus stove is moulded from silver plastic with a flame ring painted red and is shown in Plate 39.5 with the billy can lid simmering above its three metal pan supports The billy can itself has a brass metal handle.

NOT SHOWN - ice axe with flag, high altitude equipment, suckers, mess tins, knife, fork and spoon. The goggles can be seen in Plate 6.1, with all base camp accessories seen in Plate 41.2.

40. ADVENTURERS

40.1

40. ADVENTURERS

40.2

There are two versions of the basic adventurer outfits. The first, illustrated in Plate 40.1, includes a white sweater, denim trousers and tan ankle boots.

Again based on patterns from previous sets, Plate 40.2 shows the Second Issue set. This includes a blue sweater and lighter blue cotton trousers, with prominent white stitching.

(The main Polar Explorer Set also includes a black sweater to be worn underneath the anorak.)

QUARTERMASTER
- sweater
- jeans
- boots

41. POLAR EXPLORER

QUARTERMASTER

- anorak
- jersey
- over trousers
- gloves
- boots
- rucksack
- goggles
- skis
- ski sticks
- sextant

Sledge & Dog Team
- sledge
- mileometer wheel
- three husky dogs
- harnesses
- supply boxes
- ropes

Separate Equipment Cards:
- sleeping bag
- snow parka
- goggles
- supply sledge
- snow shoes
- hat
- compass
- map and case

SPECIAL FEATURES

Polar Explorer
This blue polar anorak was issued on an Accessories Card, the main Set featur[ed] a red one. Essentially the only difference between the pattern for this piece an[d] the Mountaineer's is the fur lining around the hood. The over trousers are of th[e] same colour as the anorak and have two open square pockets on the thighs. The trousers are loose and worn with two braces, which are fastened with D-hooks and linked to elastic loops underneath the anorak.

The plain sand coloured gloves are based on the original Ski Patrol pattern however the wrists are not elasticated. They are shown together with the sexta[nt] and goggles in Plate 41.1. The sextant is made from two pieces of gold plastic pinned together, allowing the sight to be moved along the curved gauge. Whi[te] arctic boots were a new design for this series and feature five triangular ridges on the sole and buckles moulded on the outside of each ankle. The grey rucksack has a single fastening strap.

Apart from the colour, the red polar gear was based on the same patterns as pieces from the Ski Patrol and Mountain Troops Sets. The skis are the exceptio[n] with their new curled D-shaped wire, a less complicated design than the figur[e] eight version on the original Ski Patrol skis. All these pieces are inscribed Hasbro ®, or Hasbro ® Hongkong. The red polar snowshoes are shown in Pla[te] 41.3. The shoe attaches to the wearer with a four-cord elastic strap. Each shoe has a Hasbro ® Japan inscription on the base.

Separate Equipment Cards
Plate 41.2 shows the blue radio transmitter and storm lamp from the Base Cam[p] Set. The radio is based on the same pattern as the green Combat version and is shown here with lid back and 2.5" silver plastic aerial extended. The storm lam[p] contains a bulb and spring. The battery required to light the lamp is inserted af[ter] unscrewing the transparent top from the cylindrical base. A wire handle is fixe[d] into two lugs in the transparent top.

The light blue polar sleeping bag can also be seen, as can an orange GI Joe map case, an ice pick and the compass. This compass is a standard size piec[e] (0.75" diameter) enclosed in a clear polyurethane casing with green PVC stra[p]

Snow Parka
Another piece from a separate accessory car[d] the basic single-breasted snow parka is mad[e] from plain fur fabric with a pale yellow nylo[n] lining, and fastens with three pairs of hook a[nd] eyes. Apart from the hood, there are no othe[r] distinguishing features such as pockets or cu[ffs]

41.2

41.3

41. POLAR EXPLORER

41.1

41.4

Sledge and Supply Boxes
The Sledge comprises four pieces of wood coloured plastic and a silver mileometer wheel, which is fastened to the rear of the main bed. The Set came complete with four supply boxes of a similar pattern to the Rivercraft pieces (see 38 Jungle Explorer). The only difference is the title on the lid, which reads 'Trans Polar Expedition'. Plate 41.4 also illustrates the red snow shoes, skis and ski sticks, the grey rucksack with its single fastening strap, the compass and the Explorer's over trousers and boots.

NOT SHOWN – the three Huskies and harnesses from the Sledge & Dog Team set.

41.5

41.6

41.7

42. UNDERWATER EXPLORER

QUARTERMASTER

- wet suit jacket
- trunks
- fins
- face mask
- depth gauge
- air cylinder
- hammer
- harpoon gun
- knife and sheath

Skin Diver:
- face mask
- snorkel
- trunks
- knife and sheath
- collecting bag

There were a number of sets issued in this series which are n[ot] featured here – the treasure hunter, underwater scooter and film unit for example. These Plates show the basic Skin Diver S[et]

SPECIAL FEATURES

Wetsuit
The blue Underwater Explorer's version of the wetsuit jacket is shown in Plate 42.3. Note the simple stitching on the main zip, the yellow AMSAC (Action Man Sub Aqua Club) paper sticker and the face on the diver's watch. A later three-piece orange wetsuit was issued based on this First Issue pattern.

Harpoon Gun and accessories
Plate 42.2 shows the golden plastic harpoon being fitted into the gun. The barrel component is painted silver and the trigger and grip section black. There are no inscriptions or markings on this piece. The sheathed knife can be seen strapped to the left leg and the yellow facemask and snorkel, navy blue nylon trunks and light blue polyurethane flippers are shown in Plate 42.1.

Air Cylinder
The air cylinder included in the Underwater Explorer Se[t] has a single silver polyurethane tank clipped onto a curved, inverted T shaped, back plate. The circular blac[k] valve at the top of the tank is connected to orange ribbe[d] hoses on either side of the black plastic mouthpiece. At [the] foot of the cylinder is a black six-finned section. Note th[e] thin orange tube clipped to the left side of the air cylind[er]

Plate 42.3 clearly illustrates the different type of ridged hose that is used on the air cylinders compared to the Fi[rst] Issue Underwater Demolition piece in Plate 11.1.

NOT SHOWN – collectors bag

114

42. UNDERWATER EXPLORER

42.1

CEREM

ONIALS
PLATES 43-49

PALITOY REG'D
ACTION OFFICIAL
man MANUAL
by Palitoy

43. GRENADIER GUARDSMAN

QUARTERMASTER

- bearskin
- jacket
- trousers
- boots
- belt
- scabbard and frog
- bayonet
- SLR

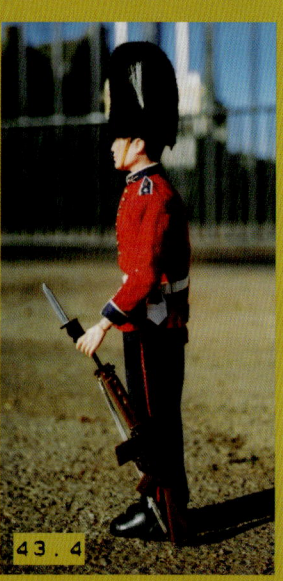

SPECIAL FEATURES

Parade Jacket and Trousers

Wearing a 2.5" high bearskin, with a white plume on the left hand side, the Guardsman is dressed in a scarlet parade jacket. Seven parts make up the chest and waist skirt alone in this complex piece. The single-breasted jacket has white piping at the front opening with eight spiked brass buttons. The close-up of the jacket in Plate 43.3 shows the crown button motif, common to all buttons of this type.

The navy stand collar is piped in white and has a bursting grenade emblem (with a silver ball representing the grenade). The blue and white fabric epaulettes also have a bursting grenade emblem and are fixed with spiked brass buttons. Cuffs are edged in blue with white piping. The rear skirt has two vertical sets of four buttons on a scalloped tail facing, the straight edges of which are sewn into the side back seams. Plate 43.2 clearly shows the component pieces of material, the curved seams on the back of the jacket, the piped central vent, and the two rows of five buttons.

The trousers are made of a thick navy material, with a thin scarlet seam stripe on each leg. They fasten with a single popper at the waist.

Belt

The three piece white PVC belt features a brass coloured buckle, with a Grenadier Guards inscription on the outside circle, and bursting grenade device on the inner circle. Two oblong brass clips connect the belt parts and two brass buckles at the end of each strap allow the belt to be adjusted.

Boots

The five-eyelet lace up parade boots are made of black polyurethane. They of a different pattern to those issued with the British Infantryman Set. Moulde stitching is neater on the toecap and there is no stitching around the heel or eyelets. These pieces are also fatter and shinier than the British Infantrymen boots and have a thinner toe cap. A Hasbro ® inscription and mould numbe can be seen on the heels, with a hole at the front of each sole.

SLR Rifle and Bayonet

The Action Man SLR (Self-Loading Rifle) is made from a single piece of chestnut coloured plastic with black painted metal work. Two S shaped wire clips fix the white six-cord elastic strap to the rifle. The length of the strap is adjusted with a square brass buckle. The shape of the protruding bayonet lu can also be seen in Plate 43.3, just below the flash suppressor.

The bayonet frog looped around the belt and the black polyurethane scabba can be seen in profile in Plate 43.4. The scabbard is moulded with a circula pin and a hole through both sides at the base. The polyurethane bayonet ha a silver blade inserted into a black handle section. The loop on the bayonet over the end of the gun barrel and there is also a slot in the base for the inver T-shaped lug.

43. GRENADIER GUARDSMAN

This set includes the Self-Loading Rifle introduced by the British Army in 1954. This 7.62mm weapon had a 20 round magazine and remained in frontline service until it was replaced by the shorter Royal Enfield 5.56mm SA80 (Side Arm 80) in 1992. The SLR was not a British design but was made originally by the Belgian firm Fabrique Nationale and designated FAL (Fusil Automatique Legere). After 1975 British SLR's used black plastic, instead of wooden components.

44. ARGYLL & SUTHERLAND HIGHLANDER

QUARTERMASTER

- glengarry
- jacket
- belt
- kilt
- sporran
- hose
- spats
- boots
- scabbard and frog
- bayonet
- SLR

SPECIAL FEATURES

From the top of the Glengarry to the spats, this set is all class.

Jacket
The short jacket includes six patterned spiked silver buttons. There are also three smaller silver buttons on the cuff, which are set off with stitched buttonholes and an unpiped V-cut section. The epaulettes are plain and fixed with a small spiked button. The stand collar and cuffs are edged in white piping. A figure of eight emblem on the collar is held in place with a loop of cotton.

The back of the jacket features curved darts with two small silver buttons at the small of the back. There are three flaps at the rear of the jacket; two have stitched yellow facings and a triple button arrangement similar to the cuffs. Three poppers fasten the jacket and at the bottom edge of the jacket front are two hooks to keep the white polyurethane belt in place.

Glengarry
This hat is made of navy blue polyurethane with a red painted pom pom at the middle of the V in the crown. A thin red and white chequered hatband is fitted into the slot at the back edge together with two black ribbons. A large silver plastic crown and laurels regimental badge is fixed on the left side of the Glengarry, as shown in Plate 44.2.

Kilt and Sporran
The kilt is woven in the Government, or Sutherland, pattern and a complex piece with an elasticated and pleated middle/rear section and plain double wrap-over front. Front sections are fastened with two poppers and a blue ribbon hem that also holds in place the two braces. The sporran is made up of a number of components, six in all: a white polyurethane belt, a black moulded pouch with three gold and white tassels threaded through it, and a curved gold plastic clip. The silver belt buckle is moulded with the regimental emblem and the belt fits through the silver metal loop shown on the right.

Hose and Spats
The red and white patterned hose have red felt tabs. The white spats are in a heavy weave fabric; they are fastened with vertical Velcro strips and a thin white six-cord elastic strap looped under the sole of the boots. See plate 44.1.

120

44. ARGYLL & SUTHERLAND HIGHLANDER

45. LIFE GUARD

QUARTERMASTER

- helmet
- tunic
- breeches
- gauntlets
- jackboots
- spurs
- belt
- cartouche belt and box
- sword and scabbard

Separate Equipment Card:
- Breastplate

The first cavalry uniform released in the Action Man range is extremely accurate in its detailing.

SPECIAL FEATURES

Breastplate
On the front of the breastplate are two pins holding the golden plastic front clasps in place. These clips are heat-sealed onto the gold coloured ribbon 'scale' straps. At the waist is a thin white polyurethane belt, with small square plastic buckle, which is fastened to two pins on the rear breastplate. The rear clasps for the breastplate straps fit into two holes in the rear plate (Plate 45.2).

Cartouche Box, Tunic and Breeches
The wide cartouche belt fastens to the box through two brass rings and features an edging strap and a square golden buckle. The black box itself is made of polyurethane with a square gold regimental badge fastened to the fl with two folded spikes. The box can be opened, the flap is held in place by small pin, which slots into a moulded hole in the body of the box. The scarl flask-cord on the cartouche belt can be clearly seen in Plate 45.1.

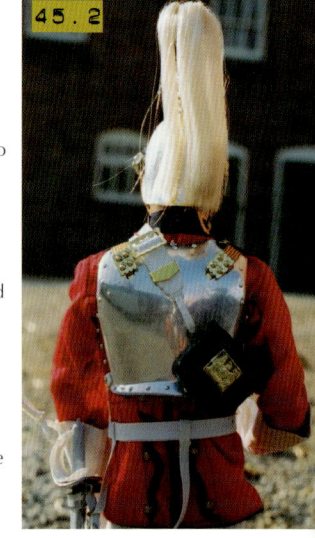

Plate 45.1 also gives a good illustration of the intricately moulded sword belt buckle, which was common to both the Life Guards and Blues & Royals Sets. Ceremonial belt buckles are made from two pieces of plastic – the buckle itself, and the base fastener. The fastene are connected to the left belt loop by a lug and the right belt loop by an L-shaped flange. This fits into a corresponding lug on the belt.

The scarlet tunic has navy piping on the seams, a blue and gold fabr standing collar flash and three blue embroidered tail facings with gold spiked brass buttons, as seen in Plate 45.3. Epaulettes are made of bl fabric with gold edging and are held in place by a golden spiked bra button. The white ribbed nylon breeches have white four-cord elastic braces and ankle loops.

Helmet
The helmet is made up of five components, plus a white nylon plum The main plastic helmet piece is chromed, with a moulded oak leaf and garter star detail sprayed gold. At each temple are circular clips, which hold the gold ribbon chinstrap in place. At the top of the cent spike is a moulded ring through which the plume is threaded. The la round pommel was glued on to keep the plume in place.

The Austrian, or Albert, helmet was introduced during the reign of Queen Victoria.

Jackboots
The black knee-length jackboots are moulded from a single piece of polyurethane topped with a pointed outer knee guard and smaller rounded inner one. Jackboots and spurs are shown in Plate 45.3.

45. LIFE GUARD

Charles II raised the Life Guards in 1660 after the Restoration and this Set depicts the modern dress uniform of the Regiment, as seen on parade in Whitehall and at royal occasions. The basis of this uniform dates back to 1843 when the Household Cavalry first started to wear the plumed dress helmet. The basic Action Man Life Guard Set did not feature the chromed plastic breastplate. This was only available on a separate Equipment Card – unless the dressed figure was bought in its distinctive triangular, Union Jack patterned box.

45.1

46. THE BLUES & ROYALS

QUARTERMASTER

- helmet
- tunic
- breeches
- gauntlets
- jackboots
- spurs
- belt
- cartouche belt and box
- sword and scabbard

Separate Equipment Card:
- Breastplate

As well as the two regiments of Life Guards, the amalgamated Blues and Royal regiments form the Sovereign's Horse Guard (regiments such as the Grenadiers are part of the Foot Guards). The main difference from the Life Guard uniform is the colour reversal of the tunic – blue with red facings, instead of red with blue facings – and the brass spike badge on the left arm.

Both Household Cavalry uniforms have shaped cuffs with gold and red chevrons fixed by a spiked brass button. Plate 46.1 is a full-length view of the uniform with its red helmet plumed helme

SPECIAL FEATURES

Spurs
The silver plastic spurs are fitted to curved black polyurethane ankle straps. These straps are handed, with a niche allowing the strap to sit true across the ankle. A looped silver ribbon passes underneath the sole of the boot and is fitte into a square lug on each side of the spur.

Sword Belt
Detail of the white PVC sword belt and scabbard slings can seen in Plate 46.2. The scabbard is made of chromed plastic and is connected to the slings by two brass rings. Inside the basket hilt of the chromed plastic sword is fixed a white polyurethane hilt guard and a pommel tassel looped throug the both the hilt and the guard. Top of the light gloss grey painted grip can just be seen.

Gauntlet Gloves
The contrast between the two types of material used for the gauntlet gloves is clearly shown in Plate 46.3. Note the wea of the golden scale breastplate straps.

46. THE BLUES & ROYALS

46.1

47. 17TH/ 21ST LANCERS

QUARTERMASTER

- helmet
- tunic
- breeches
- gauntlets
- riding boots
- spurs
- belt
- cartouche belt and box
- ceremonial cords
- lance
- lancer pennant
- regimental pennant

SPECIAL FEATURES

Lance and Pennants
The Action Man lance is made from two parts of wood coloured plastic, which are joined underneath a white polyurethane strap; the shaft is moulded to depict the contours of bamboo cane. Silver spray-painted sections are at each end – the metal base spike and the pointed tip at the top. Plate 47.1 illustrates the length of the 17" lance.

Fixed to the lance are two pennants – one with plain red and white halves denoting a lancer regiment. Below this is a square black and white regimental flag with its emblem – the skull and cross bones with the legend 'Glory' draped across it, and the 17th/21st Lancers title at the top. Plate 47.2 shows the gauntlet and pennants tied to the shaft of the lance.

Boots and Spurs
The plain riding boots are based on the same pattern as the Russian and German Soldiers of the Century pieces. The silver plastic spurs are fitted to a plain rectangular black polyurethane ankle strap with moulded buckle and a silver ribbon, which loops underneath the sole of the boot.

The double white trouser-leg stripes were particular to the 17th Lancers, an historic regiment that took part in the Charge of the Light Brigade in 1854. The 21st also had a distinguished history with three VC's awarded at Omdurman, before merging with the 17th after World War One.

Jacket and Schapska Helmet
The black and white material for this uniform is a distinctive textured fabric. The jacket has separate skirt sections below the waist and a double breasted white section above, with fourteen brass spike type buttons. Underneath this front flap, the jacket fastens with three poppers. The epaulettes are of plain white cord and fastened by a spiked brass button. Plate 47.4 is a rear view showing the plain white stand collar, the white piping on the jacket and sleeves, the central vent with two buttons in the small of the back and the scalloped tail facings with a further set of three brass buttons. Around the waist is the yellow lancer's girdle with its two red stripes. This piece is made from elasticated fabric and fastened with a popper.

All the gauntlets in the dress uniform sets are of the same pattern. Made of two different types of material, the thumb and mitt itself are made of white cotton whilst the gauntlet cuff is made of the same type of textured fabric as the jacket and trousers.

The *schapska* has a white imitation horsehair plume and an ornate gold badge crest. Moulded from white plastic, the cap comprises a black painted helmet section, two chinstrap clips, a yellow and black helmet band with a hook at the rear and a green, yellow and gold plume pin.

Cartouche
The cartouche box displays the regimental 'Death or Glory' badge. The strap is thinner than the Life Guard's and has a squarer buckle, but the brass ring and fastening arrangements are the same. The 36" yellow cords are doubled over so that they can be looped onto the hook on the schapska. There are three yellow polyurethane double loops, which keep the cords together and they are fastened to the uniform by a further metal hook on the left shoulder. The Plates clearly show how this intricate part of the uniform is worn. Note the yellow polyurethane tassels at the end of each cord.

126

47. 17TH/21ST LANCERS

Lancer regiments were first introduced into the British Army in 1816 following the trend set by the French and the Polish Lancer regiments employed in Napoleon's Vistula Legion. The British initially converted the 9th, 12th, 16th and 23rd Light Dragoons to lancer regiments and these troops adopted the distinctive fluted and square topped Polish schapska caps.

48. ROYAL MARINE DRESS UNIFORM NO 3

QUARTERMASTER

- cap
- jacket
- trousers
- boots
- belt
- scabbard and frog
- bayonet
- SLR

In comparison to some of the other ceremonial uniforms this Set is quite simple: jacket, trousers, belt, bayonet, scabbard and frog, boots, cap and an SLR rifle. Plate 48.1 provides a full view of the uniform.

SPECIAL FEATURES

Jacket
The jacket is made from heavy navy blue twill. The stand collar has two large spiked brass emblems, which denote the Marines' globe and anchor badge. Plain epaulettes have a spiked button and a rectangular bar with the initials RM. The single-breasted jacket has five spiked brass buttons and two square, pleated breast pockets; spiked brass buttons adorn both these and the plain rectangular hip pocket flaps. The back of the jacket has a centre seam and two curved da... but no vents. A close up in Plate 48.3 provides some detail of the weave on th... jacket and the pointed cuff pattern.

Belt
The belt is made from a similar heavy weave mate... to the triple stitched First Issue pieces, although ... belt buckle arrangements are different. The outer circle has the inscription 'Gibraltar, per mare, pe... terrem' (by land, by sea) and the inner circle a l... and crown device. The buckle is held in place b... two metal strips, which fold over the ends of the belt after the material has been threaded throug... the belt lugs.

Trousers and Boots
The trousers are plain with one popper. Plate 48... clearly shows the prominent red stripe. Thicker than those on other uniform sets, these cotton stripes are and double stitched. The boots are of similar pattern to the Grenadier Guardsman's.

Cap
Moulded in white polyurethane, the cap has air vents (visible in Plate 48.1). The hatband is pair... red and the peak black. Note the brass cap bad... with globe, laurel, crown and lion emblem, and the white polyurethane bayonet frog. Plate 48.3 shows the badge on the other ranks cap.

128

48. ROYAL MARINE DRESSUNIFORM NO 3

49. ROYAL HUSSAR

QUARTERMASTER

- cap
- jacket
- trousers
- shoes
- spurs
- belt
- cartouche belt and box
- sword and scabbard

The last ceremonial set to be issued was this No 1 (temperate ceremonial uniform) of the Royal Hussars (Prince of Wales O

SPECIAL FEATURES

Jacket
The navy single-breasted jacket is made from thinner, late issue material. It has a stand collar with a three feather Prince of Wales emblem in metal, and lamé 'chain mail' shoulder straps with three spiked brass buttons, denoting the rank of captain. The two rounded breast pockets are plain with scalloped flaps, fastened by spiked brass buttons. The larger hip pockets are of a similar design but without the buttons. There are five spiked buttons and three poppers on the main seam of the jacket. Note the two jacket vents underneath the shaped darts, seen in Plate 49.3.

Trousers and Shoes
The crimson trousers have two yellow seam stripes. There is a separate plain waistband, fixed with a single popper fastener.

The shoes are made from moulded black polyurethane with a Made in Hongkong inscription on the sole and two holes by the heel. The spurs were cut down Life Guard pieces, without the ankle strap pins, and are fixed aro the shoe with a loop of black four-cord elastic.

Cap and Cartouche Box
The peaked cap is made of crimson polyurethane and is based on the same mould as the British Army Officer's (see Plate 54.1). The peak and cords are painted black. There is a large metal regimental badge above the main hatba The cartouche belt is a very intricate piece with a polyurethane crimson str and gold and white stitched lacework. Over this are fixed the five silver me parts and the officer's double chain. The cartouche box shown in Plate 49. has a full metal facing. The method of fastening the belt to the box is the sa for all the Action Man ceremonial sets.

Belt, Sword and Scabbard
The sword and scabbard are of the same pattern as the Life Guard's but fea a white, instead of grey, grip and a golden, instead of white, hilt insert and ta The belt buckle is moulded with the regimental emblem and the 'Ich Dien' legend, under which is the title 'The Royal Hussar'. The belt itself and the scabbard slings are made from the same golden ribbon used on the Life Guard's breastplate. Note the length of the central scabbard sling, as seen in Plate 49.3.

130

49. ROYAL HUSSAR

REGIM

ENTALS

PLATES 50-56

The first contemporary British combat uniform to be released was for the Parachute Regiment. The famous Red Berets, were originally raised in 1940 following Churchill's call for the formation of offensive commando 'striking companies'.

50. PARACHUTE REGIMENT

QUARTERMASTER

- beret
- scarf
- camouflage jacket
- trousers
- belt and ammunition pouch
- gaitors
- boots
- bayonet and scabbard
- Colt.45 pistol and holster
- SLR Rifle

Parachute Equipment:
- Parachute
- pack helmet
- goggles

Armoury Equipment Card:
- Bren Gun/ L4A2 section weapon

SPECIAL FEATURES

Jacket and Trousers
The camouflage, or Denison jacket was originally introduced in 1941.
The Action Man version featured here has ribbed elastic cuffs, front zip, plain epaulettes, two plain square breast pockets with pointed flaps and rectangula pocket flaps on the hips, and belt loops at the waist (the ribbed cuff material can be clearly seen in Plate 50.2). To create the camouflage effect, the cream base material is overprinted with round-edged earth brown and dark green shapes. A square regimental badge, with light blue top half and maroon belo is stuck to the left arm.

The trousers are cut in the same pattern as the original Action Soldier fatigue with two rear open square pockets.

SLR Rifle and Boots
The SLR rifle is similar to the piece included in the ceremonial sets however the six-cord elastic strap is green rather than white. The black polyurethane bo are common to the British Soldiers of the Century Set.

Second Issue Beret
This polyurethane maroon beret is based on the original Green Beret mould but with the curve of the badge at the top, instead of the bottom. The red badge has an eight-pointed star and an inverted crown, see Plate 50.2.

Para Helmet and Bren Gun
Following the introduction of a real parachute in the Red Devil Set, a green chute was introduced with the same green 'folding halves' polyurethane parachute pack (see Plate 31). Included with this Parachute Equipment Set i the British pattern parachute helmet. Circular in shape, the thick green plast helmet has black polyurethane straps with a chin guard and rear neck strap fastened by a simple slot clasp.

The weapon represented here is the successor to the Bren Gun – a modified L4A using standard NATO 7.62mm ammunition. This Action Man piece, initially in duced in the Armoury series, is made of dark blue plastic with a dark brown painted butt, pistol grip and handle. The separate V-shaped bipod can be folde back along the barrel.

Other Equipment
New with the Parachute Regiment Set are the light brown textured fabric an gaiters and the green nylon muffler, or scarf. The Colt.45, holster and sand coloured pistol belt are all based on the original First Issue patterns. The ammunition pouches are from a single section Combat mould.

The scabbard was not issued with a frog. It fits loosely over the belt and is h in place by a protruding pin.

50. PARACHUTE REGIMENT

51. ROYAL MARINE

QUARTERMASTER

- beret
- jacket
- trousers
- gaitors
- boots
- belt
- pouch
- bayonet and scabbard
- sterling SMG

SPECIAL FEATURES

Combat Uniform
The basic Marine combat uniform has a jacket of the same pattern as the Parachute Regiment version but in plain light green material. Plate 51.2 provides detail of the zip front, pockets and stretch fabric cuffs. Note the brown coloured scarf just seen at the neckline. The pouch is outsize in comparison to the figure and is made of a darker earth coloured material with a single silver buckle. Plain green trousers have a left thigh pocket with a pointed flap.

The anklet gaiters pictured are from the British Infantryman Set in the Soldiers of the Century series, and are not the brown fabric wrap-around type issued with this Marines Set (see also Plate 50. Parachute Regiment).

Third Issue Beret
The green polyurethane beret illustrated is a third issue version and has a more rounded shape than the original issue; a first issue piece was moulded on the same pattern as the Green Beret version. The second issue version was made of cloth with a metal globe, laurel leaf and crown badge.

Sterling Submachine Gun
The Sterling submachine gun replaced the Sten in 1953 and remained in British service for over four decades. The commonly used banana-shaped magazine held 34 rounds but the Action Man piece depicted is the shorter straight version. Made from a single mould, this is one of the last elastic strap weapons. The strap rings are silver and the four-cord elastic strap is itself thinner than other weapon straps.

Belt
The belt is of the double-thickness heavy weave fabric commonly used for these pieces. Buckles are here held in place by metal loops which mean that the length of the belt cannot be adjusted (First Issue belts have adjustable plastic loops).

51.2

51. ROYAL MARINE

51.1

52. ROYAL MARINE MOUNTAIN AND ARCTIC

QUARTERMASTER

- cap
- goggles
- snow suit
- gloves
- boots
- belt
- pouches
- bayonet and scabbard
- skis
- ski sticks
- white SLR

SPECIAL FEATURES

Snow Suit
The third Marines uniform to be introduced is a simpler version of the First Issue Ski Patrol outfit. The white snow suit is plain with draw cords at the skirt and hood only, two popper fasteners and no pockets. Note the thinner ski suit material in Plate 52.2. The plain trousers are fastened by a single draw cord and do not have elasticated ankles. The white boots are common with the Polar Explorer Set.

The heavy weave pouch is clearly shown in Plate 52.1, together with the white plastic version of the SLR with its white elastic strap and black spray painted metal parts. This pouch is similar to the green version shown in Plate 51.1. These later issue goggles have a plain green polyurethane strap.

Skis
These skis shown in 52.2 are based on the original Ski Patrol pattern, with a Hasbro Hongkong ® inscription. This version has a metal plate and single wire D loop just like the Polar Explorer pieces. The First Issue pattern white handled ski sticks are also shown. These retain the silver spiked ends but have white PVC straps. Hasbro ® is inscribed on the circular section.

52.2

138

52. ROYAL MARINE – MOUNTAIN AND ARCTIC

52.1

53. ROYAL MARINE EXPLORATION TEAM

QUARTERMASTER

- life raft
- oars
- life vest
- bush hat
- crash helmet
- radio set and headphones
- jungle knife
- snake bite kit
- cine camera
- rope

Fourth in the Royal Marines series, this is a later issue set from 1975. The basic uniform from the Royal Marines Exploration Team is also used in the last issue Soldiers of the World Australian Jungle Fighter (see Plate 63.2). Note the full brim on the campaign hat, which is not turned up, and the standard pattern Jungle Knife. The shirt is made from a different material to the trousers – the weave of the fabrics can be compared in Plate 63.1.

SPECIAL FEATURES

Snake Bite Kit
Attached to the belt is the brown polyurethane snake bite kit pouch, with a lug at either side allowing the belt to be threaded through. The basic pouch is subdivided in two, with a green paper sticker on the front (this pouch is also common with the GI Joe Japanese Infantryman Set).

Life Raft, Life Vest and Crash Helmet
A life raft and orange crash helmet were issued with this Set. The life raft, as shown in Plate 53.2, is considerably larger than the original Survival piece – 15" long compared to 10" – and can accommodate two figures rather than one. This larger version still features the four oar loops, a transparent air valve at the stern and the semi-circular flap at the front for attaching the anchor. Two black oars with yellow tips were issued with this Set.

The orange plastic helmet is based on the original Scramble pattern but has no stencilled writing. It fastens with a simple black polyurethane strap. The life vest is also based on the original pattern Scramble piece, but with a thinner foam fill and a different stencilled logo. It has a Made in Hongkong inscription in the centre of the bottom seal.

Cine Camera
The camera, seen in Plate 53.1, is made from black plastic and has a Hasbro ® Hongkong inscription on the bottom left hand side.

NOT SHOWN – radio (see Plate 18.4)

140

53. ROYAL MARINE EXPLORATION TEAM

53.1

54. BRITISH ARMY OFFICER

QUARTERMASTER

- cap
- jacket
- trousers
- shirt
- tie
- socks
- shoes
- Sam Browne belt
- swagger stick

SPECIAL FEATURES

Jacket and Trousers
This staff officer wears another quality uniform, as the thick weave on the material shows in Plate 54.1. The chestnut brown jacket is made from 21 pieces of cloth. It has two large plain rectangular-flap hip pockets and pleated breast pockets with pointed flaps. All pocket flaps are fastened with silver spike buttons and there are a further four buttons to the jacket front. The open collar is decorated with two small silver spike regimental badges - 'Death or Glory' lancers' insignia. The epaulettes are plain with a single silver spike button fastening and separate pointed cuffs are stitched to each sleeve. A rear view in Plate 54.2 shows the back seam and two darts at either side of the central ver Also shown is the plastic wood-coloured swagger stick.

The trousers are fastened with a single popper and have no particular distinguishing features.

Shirt and Tie
Underneath the jacket is an ill-fitting light brown shirt, with two poppers at the front and one on each cuff. The brown tie is mad of the same type of textured fabric as the 17th/21st Lancers unifor and is held in place by a white four-cord elastic loop.

Sam Browne Belt and Cap
A complex item, the brown Sam Browne belt is made from seven pieces of PVC, four polyurethane pins and four metal parts. The sash buckle can be clearly seen in Plate 54.1, togeth with the square buckle, which threads over the belt and is helc in place by two pins at the rear. The standard pattern peaked c has a red hat band and a large silver spiked regimental badge

Shoes and Socks
In brown polyurethane with a mould number and Hasbro ® Hongkong inscription, the shoes are worn over three-quarter length brown socks. These socks are elasticated, made of the same material as those of the original Australian Jungle Fighter.

54. BRITISH ARMY OFFICER

55. ROYAL MILITARY POLICE

QUARTERMASTER

- cap
- jacket
- trousers
- shirt and tie
- belt
- MP armband
- boots
- truncheon
- Sterling SMG
- signs

This Redcap is armed with a Sterling submachine gun but some catalogue pictures show a Sten included in the Set.

SPECIAL FEATURES

Uniform
The M.P.'s uniform is similar to, if plainer than, the Army Officer's and is made from brighter green material. There are no hip pockets, just unbuttoned rectangular flaps. Collar badges are of a crown/laurel leaf design. In all there are eight buttons on the jacket as the epaulettes are buttoned whilst the jacket sleeves are plain. The trousers are also plain and fasten with a single popper.

A rear view in Plate 55.2 shows some detail of the jacket's centre back seam and the two shaped seams at either side of the central vent. The red cotton MP armband is fastened by a single popper.

The shirt in this Set is of a lighter green than the Army Officer's. The elastic tie loop is seen in close up in Plate 55.3. Also shown is the embossed silver spike badge.

Forage Cap
The peaked forage cap is moulded in red polyurethane. It has a navy band and a steeply angled peak, spray-painted in black. The spiked cap badge has the initials 'EIIR' encircled by laurel leaves and a crown. Note the moulded texture of the cap and the central seam. Plate 55.3 also shows the white plastic truncheon with red PVC loop.

NOT SHOWN: paper sticker sergeant's rank stripes.

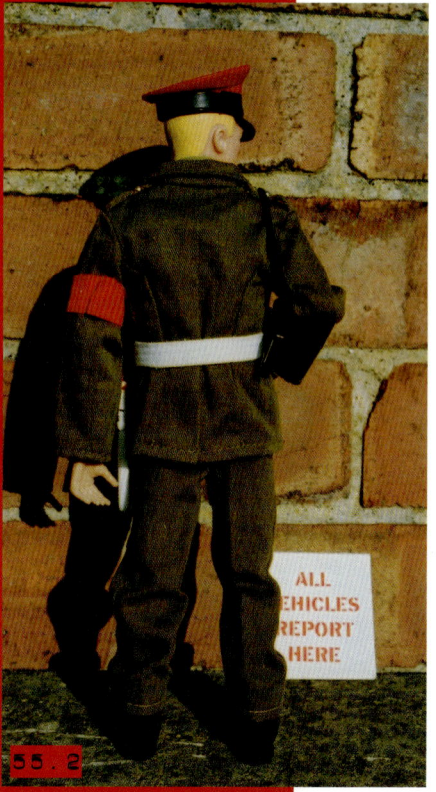

55. ROYAL MILITARY POLICE

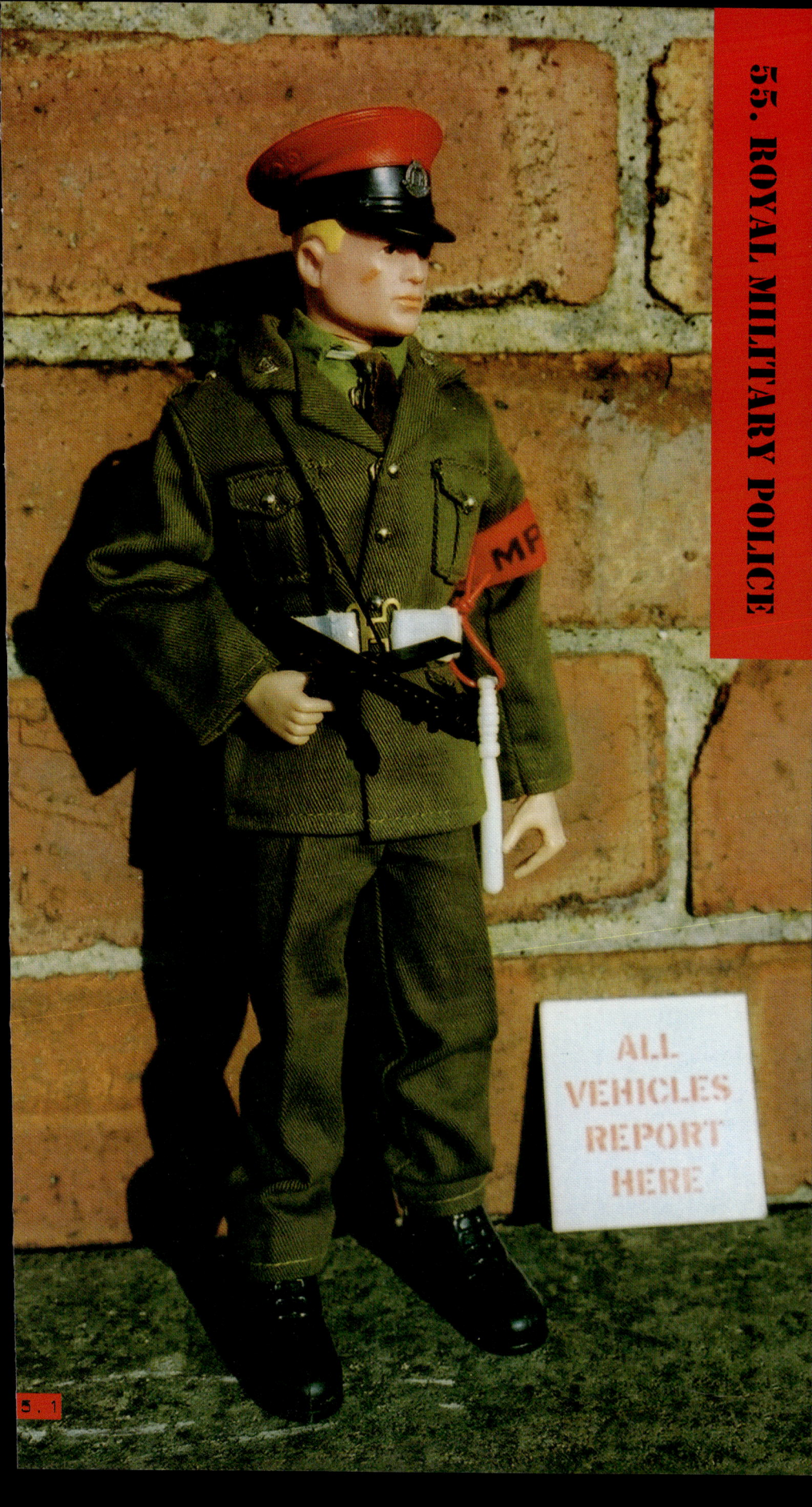

56. DISPATCH RIDER

QUARTERMASTER

- crash helmet
- goggles
- leather jerkin
- battledress jacket and trousers
- gauntlets
- belt
- riding boots

SPECIAL FEATURES

Jerkin
This Set is another World War Two era uniform. The long leather waistcoat w originally introduced by the British during World War One. The Action Man piece shown here is made of three pieces of fabric and has three metal butto poppers. Plate 56.1 shows the texture of the fabric jerkin,

Battledress and Breeches
This Set also heralded the next issue of battledress for the British soldier. Cu the same pattern as the first Soldiers of the Century sets, the tunic is made o thinner material in a richer shade of brown. Although there is the same cros sword unit flash on the left arm, there are no rank chevrons or medal ribbo The breeches are a new design, cut to a wide-thigh jodhpur pattern. Plate 5 provides a good view of the cut of the breeches.

Helmet and Boots
Also featured in this Set are a black pair of riding boots and a plain gree riding helmet with a simple black polyurethane strap fastening into the lower set of four holes in each the side of the helmet. All these pieces a from patterns used in previous sets. The boots are duller than the origin Soldiers of the Century counterparts, and have odd sized mould numbe on the heels: a small 1 on the left boot and a larger 2 on the right.

Gauntlets
Brown textured fabric gauntlets are tucked under the arm in Plate 56.3. These gauntlets are cut to the same pattern as those included in the ceremonial sets but use only one type of fabric – a similar material to t used for the jerkin.

146

56. DISPATCH RIDER

SOLDIER OF THE WORLD

PLATES 57-72

With the demise of the First Issue sets and then the Soldiers of the Century series, some of the uniforms were revamped in later Soldiers of the World and Frontliner sets. Some of the pieces from earlier sets were also made available on equipment cards, the Quartermasters Stores for example. By this stage the bullet holes from the Action Man logo had been dropped and later Equipment Store cards were issued with the word 'Action' in blue instead of the original black. This chapter therefore concentrates on the later versions of the First Issue uniforms and also illustrates some of the later issue weapons, which have polyurethane straps rather than corded elastic. Some uniforms disappeared altogether, such as the Green Beret, others were unchanged, for example the French Resistance Fighter, and these are therefore not shown again.

ACTION man
INTELLIGENCE MANUAL
TOP SECRET

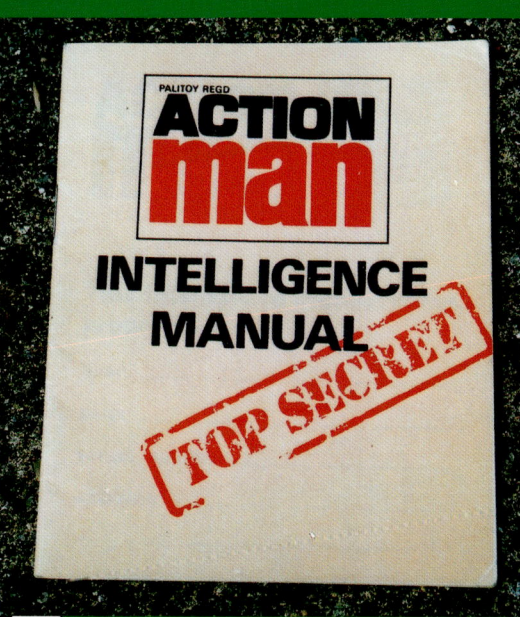

MORSE CODE

57. FRENCH FOREIGN LEGIONNAIRE

SPECIAL FEATURES

Greatcoat
The navy blue serge M1877 greatcoat is double breasted, with two rows of four spiked brass buttons. First Issue versions of this Set are made from a lighter horizon blue material. The cut of the greatcoat is modelled in the French style – skirts fixed up at the side with a further pair of brass spiked buttons, in marching order. The greatcoat has a round-edged collar and fastens with two poppers. The centre back seam ends in a large vent. The plain sleeves are single stitched. Also shown are the black standard pattern ankle boots, and plain white single-poppered trousers.

Lebel Rifle and Bayonet
Plate 57.1 illustrates an 8mm 1886 Lebel rifle, the longest rifle supplied for Action Man at 9". The cruciform needle bayonet with the recurved quillon is also the longest bayonet at 2.5". The strap on the rifle is fixed with two lugs at the butt and the first silver painted barrel ring. A square brass buckle on the black four-cord elastic strap allows it to be adjusted.

Undershirt and Bodybelt
The plain white collarless undershirt has three-quarter length sleeves. The fuction of the navy blue silk body belt is to provide warmth on cold desert nights and support the wearer's back. It fastens with two poppers. Both can be seen in Plate 57.2.

QUARTERMASTER
- kepi
- coat
- sash
- shirt
- trousers
- boots
- belt with pouches
- canteen & waterbottle
- bayonet and scabbard
- backpack
- Lebel rifle

Armoury Equipment Card:
- Vickers Machine Gun

Water bottle
The Horizon Blue M1877 2-litre water bottle is moulded in the traditional French pattern with two spouts. The bottle is connected to the black polyurethane strap by a rectangular lug. The buff painted corks are clearly visible in Plate 57.1.

Pack
Lying on the ground in Plate 57.2 is the sand coloured pack. Made from heavy weave material, this piece has two black six-cord elastic straps. The pointed flap is fastened to the body of the pack with a square piece of, then revolutionary, Velcro.

57. FRENCH FOREIGN LEGIONNAIRE

57.1

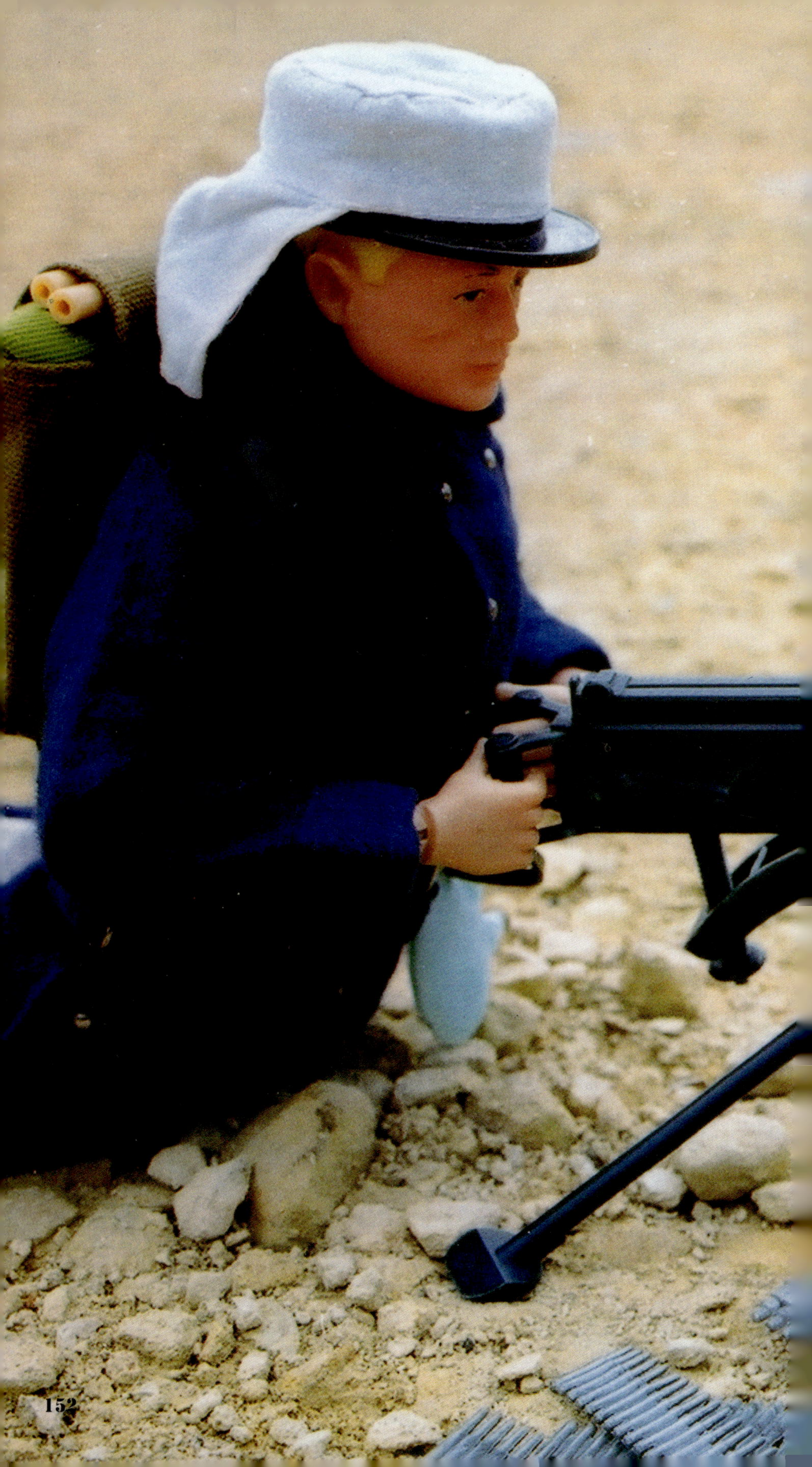

57. FRENCH FOREIGN LEGIONNAIRE

Kepi
Plate 57.4 profiles the navy polyurethane kepi with separate white cotton cover and neck flap. The top of the kepi is painted red and is flat, not slanted like the original Action Soldier's piece.

Vickers Machine Gun

> The Vickers machine gun was a British design introduced in 1912, which remained in service until 1966. With a rate of fire of 450 .303 rounds per minute, the Vickers is a water-cooled weapon with a square water container (not supplied with the Action Man piece). This type of weapon is very similar to the 1910 Maxim model used extensively by the French and the Russians.

The Action Man weapon from the Armoury series is moulded from dark blue plastic with a brown painted barrel. Four components make up the tripod, all moulded in dark blue plastic. A screw adjuster at the base of the body of the gun can be used to alter the angle of the barrel. Each gun was supplied with one silver polyurethane ammunition belt inscribed Hasbro ® Hongkong.

Belt and Pouches
The black polyurethane belt and M1892 'Y' braces include three ammunition pouches – two at the front and one at centre back – plus a bayonet frog for the plain scabbard. Each of the front M1888 pattern pouches holds four packets of eight rounds, and the back pouch holds three packets. The Action Man piece is made from a single mould with a brass ring inserted into a loop on each strap. The belt buckle fastens at the front with a tongue and lug arrangement.

Note the pup tent pole sections seen in the backpack.

57.4

58. LATE ISSUE GERMAN STORMTROOPER

QUARTERMASTER

- helmet
- tunic and trousers
- marching boots
- cartridge belt
- field pack
- grenades
- Luger pistol and holster
- 'Schmeisser' MP38/40 submachine gun
- Iron Cross

SPECIAL FEATURES

Uniform
The major difference between this Soldiers of the World Set and the First Issue version is the quality of the material. Plate 58.1 provides a good example of this, as emphasised by the contrast between the breast eagle ribbon and the jacket material (compare this Plate with Plate 16.1.) The other major differences are the breast pockets which are square in this set, rather than rounded, and the paper helmet shield stickers which replace the First Issue transfers. Plate 58.2 is a good illustration of the thinner breast eagle badge.

'Schmeisser' MP38/40 Submachine Gun
By this stage most Action Man weapons had polyurethane straps. The front strap attachment on the MP38/40 has moved from the end to the base of the barrel. The strap in Plate 58.1 is the black one produced for the set.

58.2

58. LATE ISSUE GERMAN STORMTROOPER

58.1

59. 'COLDITZ' GERMAN STORMTROOPER

QUARTERMASTER

- helmet
- tunic and trousers
- marching boots
- cartridge belt
- field pack
- grenades
- Luger pistol and holster
- 'Schmeisser' MP38 submachine gun
- Iron Cross

Following the BBC television series 'Colditz' in the early 1970's, a new German Infantryman set was introduced.

SPECIAL FEATURES

Tunic
The cut of the tunic remains the same as the First Issue version but the material is thin and shiny in a deep shade of bottle green. The breast eagle collar patches are made of fabric stickers rather than embroidered ribbon and the red *waffenfarbe* are of red textured fabric rather than the sewn piping of the earlier issue sets. A cheaper plastic is used for the buttons, which are now transparent and in a lighter shade of green. Note the absent swastika on the left helmet shield.

The epaulettes are now unhemmed, as seen in Plate 59.2.

59. 'COLDITZ' GERMAN STORMTROOPER

59.1

60. LAST ISSUE GERMAN INFANTRYMAN

SPECIAL FEATURES

Tunic
This last issue German uniform is the most historically accurate. *The feldbluse is cut with an open collar, and features white infantry waffenfarbe on the collar patches and epaulettes.* As this was a last issue uniform, the edges of the pockets are not turned under and hemmed. The pleats on the pockets are now only represented by lines of stitching instead of the folded material from earlier issue uniforms. Ten silver buttons on the tunic are of the metal spiked variety. In general, this is a far simpler uniform than the previous stormtrooper uniforms – there are no shaping darts in the back and the trousers have no elastic foot loops.

Mauser KAR98K, Cartridge Belt and 'Y' Straps
The Mauser KAR98K bolt action rifle was the standard Wehrmacht weapon of World War Two. It held a magazine of five 7.92mm bullets and was based on an original weapon introduced into service in 1898. Moulded from a single piece of brown plastic, the Action Man piece has spray painted black metal parts. There are no inscriptions and, as a late issue piece, this rifle was only made with polyurethane straps. Note the strap pin under the base of the barrel.

At the end of the front straps in Plate 60.3 are the three bullet pouches for the Mauser. On the left side of the belt is the bayonet frog and on the right the attachment for the water bottle. The bayonet scabbard is slotted into the frog; the bayonet itself is moulded from the same pattern as the French Resistance Fighter's knife (see Plate 18.3).

60.2

QUARTERMASTER

- helmet
- tunic and trousers
- marching boots
- cartridge belt and Y straps
- waterbottle
- bayonet and scabbard
- grenades
- Kar 98k rifle

The water bottle is attached with a vertical strap; made of straw-coloured polyurethane, the bottle is moulded with the cup on top. A rear view in Plate 60.3 details the black moulded polyurethane 'Y' straps.

The belt buckle is fastened by simply slotting the ends of the polyurethane belt through the lugs, where they are held in place by moulded studs.

Insignia
The cloth breast eagle is glued to the tunic; again note the absent swastika in the circular wreath.

60.3

60. LAST ISSUE GERMAN INFANTRYMAN

61. LATE ISSUE RUSSIAN INFANTRYMAN

QUARTERMASTER

- shapka fur lined hat
- jacket and trousers
- marching boots
- belt
- anti tank grenades
- ammo box
- DP light machine gun
- bipod
- magazine
- Order of Lenin

After the demise of the Soldiers of the Century series, only parts of the Russian Infantryman set could be obtained on a variety of Quartermasters Store uniform and equipment cards.

SPECIAL FEATURES

Tunic and Belt
The rear view in Plate 61.2 illustrates the lighter colour of the uniform material used in the late issue tunic. It also provides some detail of the shaping darts, button arrangements, and 'pebble' moulding on the PVC belt. Detail on the belt buckle is shown in Plate 61.1.

Cap
The peaked cap in Plate 61.1 finally replaced the fur *shapka-ushanka* piece. Note the hammer and sickle cap badge, which is from an original fur *shapka* (later issue caps were only issued with a paper sticker badge).

Plate 61.2 allows a comparison of a later issue *shapka* cap with the First Issue cap seen in Plate 17.1. Note the thinner and darker fur fabric used in this later issue piece

61.2

160

61. LATE ISSUE RUSSIAN INFANTRYMAN

62. LATE ISSUE BRITISH INFANTRYMAN

QUARTERMASTER

- helmet
- battle dress tunic and trousers
- ammunition boots
- gaiters
- belt
- gasmask and bag
- canteen and cover
- Sten sub machine gun
- magazine
- Victoria Cross

SPECIAL FEATURES

Battledress
The Second Issue battledress shown in Plate 62.1 is of a lighter material and greener hue. The fabric is of relatively poor quality and is less durable than f First Issue pieces. However there are no differences to the pattern or insignia.

A later issue uniform, with no NCO (Non Commissioned Officer) stripes, is shown in Plate 62.1. It is of a thinner denim material, in contrast to the heavy diagonal weave shown in Plates 19.1 or 62.2. Note the plain epaulettes and the jacket waistband. The trousers have an open square pocket on the right thigh and elasticated ankle tabs.

Lee Enfield and Webbing
The polyurethane strapped Lee Enfield No.4 Mk1 is shown in Plate 62.1. Introduced by the British in 1942, the original .303 bolt action rifle held a ten round magazine. The Action Man piece is moulded from a single piece of chestnut plastic, with spray painted dark blue metal parts with a Made in Hongkong inscription on the butt a mould number on the magazine. Also shown is the moulded buff polyurethane 1937 pattern webbing with ammunition pouches (the original could hold up to 50 .303 rounds in each pouch). This type of belt fastens with a tongue on the right sid fitting into a lug on the left.

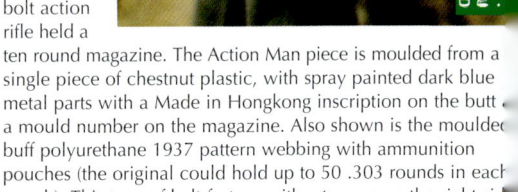

Equipment
The rear view in Plate 62.3 shows some more detail of the cr over webbing straps, the water bottle, the entrenching tool an knife. The water bottle is the same pattern as the First Issue vers but is moulded from green instead of silver plastic. The green version represents the felt covering of the 1908 pattern bottle, shown here enclosed in open strapwork. Note also the water bottle cover shown in Plate 62.2.

On the left of Plate 62.3 is a plain bayonet frog through whic slots the brown plastic scabbard. The silver polyurethane knif modelled on the pattern of a commando knife and cannot be f on to the rifle. Also shown is the entrenching tool cover contair the black polyurethane entrenching tool head (See also Plate 2 The shaft of the entrenching tool is used as a pin to hold the front and the back of the cover together.

62.3

62. LATE ISSUE BRITISH INFANTRYMAN

63. LATE ISSUE AUSTRALIAN JUNGLE FIGHTERS

QUARTERMASTER

Second Issue:
- bush hat
- shirt
- trousers
- belt
- boots
- machete and sheath
- Sterling Submachine Gun

Third Issue:
- bush hat
- shirt
- trousers
- belt
- boots
- ammunition belt
- flamethrower
- machete and sheath
- Patchett Machine Carbine

Last Issue:
- bush hat
- shorts
- boots
- Thompson SubMachine gun

SECOND ISSUE

An example of the Second Issue Quartermasters Stores khaki jacket can be seen in Plate 63.1. Note the plain breast pockets and the flaps representing the hip pockets. The actual hip pockets of the First Issue version are no longer present, and the back of the jacket is plain with no pleats or separate shoulder yoke. Plain khaki trousers are cut to the same pattern as the Action Soldier denims and have two square open back pockets.

The brown combat ankle boots are moulded on the standard pattern. Both campaign hat and jungle knife are identical to earlier issue pieces.

THIRD ISSUE

The Soldiers of the World Set in Plate 63.2 represents a distinct change of uniform. It is based on the same pattern as the Royal Marines Jungle Exploration S Made from a closer weave material, the trousers have a deep rectangular thi pocket on the left leg, with a pointed flap. The matching belt has a plain square brass buckle and the machete sheath threads over this. The shirt is made of a looser weave material. There are no embellishments to the basic shir pattern: plain collar, plain back and three poppers on the single-breasted shir front. Its square pleated breast pockets have a plain rectangular flap and the separate cuffs are poppered.

Ammunition Belts and Sterling Submachine Gun
The Third Issue included two black polyurethane ammunition belts. They are connected by two sets of holes and pins underneath the plain section, shown here at the left shoulder in Plate 63.2. Also included was the Sterling s machine gun with a triangular butt – shown in Plate 63.2 deputising fo the very similar 1941 Australian Patchett 9mm machine carbine.

LAST ISSUE

The Last Issue Desert Fighter set shown in Plate 63.3 has minimal accoutrements. The only new item is a pair of plain green shorts, fastened by a single rivet type popper. The campaign hat and the bro combat ankle boots are identical to earlier issue pieces.

Thompson Submachine Gun
The weapon shown in Plate 63.1 is the .45 calibre American Thompso M1928 submachine gun included with the Last Issue Desert Fighter. Th Action Man piece is made from dark blue plastic with chestnut painted wooden furniture and has a black polyurethane strap and a 20 round box magazine. There is a Made in Hong Kong inscription on the butt.

Also shown in Plate 63.2 are two First Issue ammunition boxes made from green plastic with yellow stencilled lettering. Handles on the lid are connected to the box by square brass links. The flame thrower issued in the Third Issue Set was identical to the camouflaged version included with the First Issue (see Plate 20.2).

NOT SHOWN: flame thrower.

63. LATE ISSUE AUSTRALIAN JUNGLE FIGHTERS

63.1

64. MINE DETECTION

QUARTERMASTER

- helmet
- jacket
- mine detector
- mines

This Set not only includes the mine detector shown in Plate 23.2 but also a complete uniform and A1 pattern helmet, with a skull and crossbones sticker badge.

SPECIAL FEATURES

Jacket
The jacket has an open collar and plain epaulettes and fastens with three poppers. Plate 64.1 shows the back of the jacket, which is plain with a printed white symbol and 'Mine Clearing' inscription. There are no cuffs or buttons; two square breast pockets with rectangular flaps are sewn onto the front of the jacket.

Mines
The three metallic discs shown can be used to complete the circuit on the mine detection unit.

Also shown is a First Issue green plastic entrenching tool, extended from its folded carrying position. Note too the bayonet, used by mine hunters to dig out discovered mines, and the combat boots with ridges around the outside of the soles.

64. MINE DETECTION

65. LAST ISSUE MOUNTAIN & ARCTIC UNIFORM

QUARTERMASTER

- cap
- goggles
- snow suit
- gloves
- boots
- belt and pouches
- pouches
- water bottle
- bayonet and scabbard
- skis
- ski sticks
- white SLR rifle

The last issue version of this uniform. Plate 65.1 provides a full length view of the complete set.

SPECIAL FEATURES

Skis
The main difference is the safer, if less authentic, blunted all-white ski sticks. The skis are simplified Ski Patrol pattern pieces with two T-shaped plastic pin either side of the foot plate, used to loop elastic bands around the boot.

65.2

Equipment

The white polyurethane 1958 pattern equipment was issued in Combat Equipment Fighting Order, as shown in Plate 65.2: two separate square 'kidney' pouches (worn over the small of the back), two rectangular ammunition pouches and a water bottle holder. The white handled bayon and scabbard complete the harness. Note the white plastic rifle strap for t SLR and the strapping on the pouch and cape carrier. The late issue snow goggles, in plain green plastic with pin and polyurethane straps, can be seen in Plate 65.1.

A rear view of the equipment in Plate 65.3 shows the shoulder yoke with U-shaped moulded loop. Two vertical straps connect to the waist belt and the moulded canteen holder on the right. The square pouches fasten onto the main webbing with side straps and a central strap between the pouch Underneath is a moulded cape carrier, part of the main harness. It fastens two separate straps, which fit into lugs on the ammunition pouches.

Note the shape of the hood when worn.

65.3

65. LAST ISSUE MOUNTAIN AND ARTIC

65.1

66. LATE ISSUE PARACHUTE REGIMENT

QUARTERMASTER

- beret
- scarf
- camouflage jacket
- trousers
- belt and pouches
- gaiters
- boots
- bayonet and scabbard
- SLR Rifle

An example of the matching tunic and camouflage trousers that were issued with later Equipment Cards.

SPECIAL FEATURES

Camouflage Uniform
The green version of the 1958 pattern equipment is shown, together with the ammunition pouches. The buckle arrangements on the belt include a simple arrow shaped tongue at the end of the right belt strap, which fits into a lug on the left.

There are several versions of the Para uniform and further details of later issue camouflaged jackets accompanying Plates 105.1 and 105.2.

Beret
Also shown is a late issue beret with a chromed plastic winged parachute regimental badge 'riveted' to the beret. This type of beret is more circular and flat than the previous First Issue 'Green Beret' pattern.

66. LATE ISSUE PARACHUTE REGIMENT

67. LATE ISSUE ROYAL MARINE

QUARTERMASTER

- beret
- scarf
- camouflage jacket and trousers
- belt and pouches
- boots
- bayonet and scabbard
- SLR rifle

SPECIAL FEATURES

Camouflage Uniform
This set incorporates a complete two-piece camouflage pattern uniform, based on the same weight and style of material as the Internationals series' German paratrooper. The profile in Plate 67.1 shows the thigh pocket with its pointed flap. This late issue style uniform is not hemmed and the pocket flap has been strengthened using a form of stiffener not found on other parts of the uniform. The jacket is fastened with three poppers at the front opening, and a single popper at each separately stitched cuff. Note the gold spike buttons and the unhemmed pocket flap.

The standard Action Man camouflage print is different to the sworling style of (DPM) Disruptive Pattern Material actually used by the British forces.

Third Issue Beret
Plate 67.2 shows the other set of the third issue beret, with plastic Royal Marines globe and crown badge.

Rifle
The SLR rifle shown here is a First Issue type with a six-cord green elastic strap and wire S clips.

67.2

172

67. LATE ISSUE ROYAL MARINE

68. LATE ISSUE ROYAL MILITARY POLICE

QUARTERMASTER

- cap
- jacket and trousers
- shirt
- tie
- belt
- MP armband
- boots
- truncheon
- Sterling Sub Machine Gun
- signs

SPECIAL FEATURES

Uniform
The main difference between this Frontliners Set and the earlier version is the quality of the uniform material. As shown here, the material is much thinner - more akin to tropical kit than the temperate weight of the uniform shown in Plate 55.3.

The later period armband issued with this set is a cheaper version – textured fabric on a PVC base with one small pin type popper.

68. LATE ISSUE RMP

68.1

69. LATE ISSUE TANK COMMANDERS

SPECIAL FEATURES

Jacket
A British tanker wearing a Quartermasters Stores issue jacket with a zip front shown in Plate 69.1. Later issue jackets are made in a double-breasted style, with two poppers instead of a zip. The type of jacket shown here is plainer than the Armoured Car Commander's piece shown in Plate 28.1, with no neck strap, epaulettes, cuff fur, slash pockets or intricate back stitching.

In all, there were four different styles issued. One in the same colour as that Plate 69.1, a thinner, darker brown PVC version and one each in green and navy blue. Plate 69.4 is a close up view of the late issue navy blue double-breasted jacket with three popper fastening. Plate 69.3 illustrates an example of the green PVC version. This fastens with three poppers and is worn closed the neck. Note the thin fur on the collar, plain cuffs and epaulettes.

The rear view in Plate 69.2 shows the simple pattern of the jacket. Note also the thigh pocket on the left trouser leg.

Royal Tank Regiment Beret
The Royal Tank Regiment beret has a badge with a World War One rhomboi shaped tank in the centre of a laurel leaf and crowned circle. This black bere is moulded on the later issue pattern (see Plate 69.1).

Jerry Can
The green polyurethane jerry can in Plate 69.2 is from the Workshop Accessories Set. Note the separate black stopper cap.

Headphones
The headphones have silver ear pieces riveted to a black polyurethane head clip and a metal mike stem connected to a silver polyurethane mouth piece. The wire on the right earphone ends in a pin, which can be connected to the outsize Field Radio Pack (not shown). Headphones are shown worn around the neck in Plate 69.1.

Also included in the Tank Commander Set are the standard pattern binoculars, flare pistol, sand coloured pistol belt, holster and M1911 Colt A1.45. All are made with more economic materials. The binoculars have a black polyurethane strap with a pin and loop fastening instead of the single-cord elastic of the First Issue.

QUARTERMASTER
- beret
- jacket
- trousers
- boots
- headphone set
- binoculars
- flare gun
- pistol belt
- Colt .45 and holster

69. LATE ISSUE TANK COMMANDERS

69.4

70. LATE ISSUE MEDIC

QUARTERMASTER

- helmet
- jacket and trousers
- armband
- stretcher
- flag
- stethoscope
- crutch
- first aid kit

SPECIAL FEATURES

Uniform
A far simpler set than the First Issue version, with a plain green jacket and trousers, armband and a white polyurethane helmet with transparent Red Cr[oss] sticker badge.

The close up view in Plate 70.2 shows the plain breast pocket and simple cu[ffs] of the open necked shirt, which has two front buttons.

Equipment
The amount of equipment is als[o] reduced in this set and of simp[le] design. The stretcher now has j[ust] the side handle poles and a thi[n]ner fabric sling than the First Issue version. A white version o[f] the First Issue ammunition box has a Red Cross sticker. First Iss[ue] items that remained unchanged are the stethoscope, the crutch and the flag, now with a 'full' Red Cross.

70.2

178

70. LATE ISSUE MEDIC

70.1

71. LAST ISSUE MEDIC

QUARTERMASTER

- helmet
- jacket and trousers
- belt
- first aid pouch
- armband
- stethoscope
- first aid kit
- life support pack

SPECIAL FEATURES

Uniform
A completely new, all white uniform, this set illustrates a pair of four-eyelet white ankle boots. The close up in Plate 71.2 details the white smock-type doctor's tunic, which is fastened by two poppers at the centre back. The stand collar has one button. A square open pocket is the only other distinguishing feature of this otherwise plain uniform.

Equipment
This late Emergency series Set includes a proliferation of red crosses – on the helmet, First Aid box and armband as before, but now also on the breast pocket and the First Aid pouch. On the floor is the white plastic oblong life support pack with its paper sticker control panel. Plate 71.2 illustrates the stethoscope and white ribbed polyurethane belt with 'pin through the hole' fastening, as shown. The First Aid pouch is made of similar material and is based on the same pattern as the piece first issued with the Royal Marines Exploration Team Set (see Plate 53.1). A paper red cross emblem is stuck to the front.

71.2

180

71. LAST ISSUE MEDIC

71.1

INTERNA

Recognise your ranks

		GERMANY	FRANCE
GENERAL OFFICERS		general, lieutenant general, major general, brigadier	marshal, general, lieutenant general, major general, brigadier
FIELD OFFICERS		colonel, lieutenant colonel, major	colonel, lieutenant colonel, major
JUNIOR OFFICERS		captain, 1st lieutenant, 2nd lieutenant	captain, 1st lieutenant, 2nd lieutenant
WARRANT & NON-COMMISSIONED OFFICERS		WO class 1, WO class II, Qtr. master sergeant, staff sergeant, sergeant	WO class 1, WO class II, staff sergeant, 1st sergeant, sergeant
APPOINTMENTS		corporal, lance corporal	senior corporal, corporal

182

TIONALS

PLATES 72-78

Issued without equipment, the six uniforms in this chapter were all released on their own Internationals Equipment Cards. Some, like the American Paratrooper and the Afrika Korps, were also issued as full sets; others, like the Russian Infantryman and the UN Soldier, were unique to these equipment cards with only the helmet, jacket, trousers and boots being issued on blister packs.

U.S.A.	RUSSIA
general of the army	marshal
general — lieutenant general	general — lieutenant general
major general — brigadier	major general — brigadier
colonel	colonel
lieutenant colonel — major	lieutenant colonel — major
captain	captain — senior lieutenant
1st lieutenant — 2nd lieutenant	lieutenant — 2nd lieutenant
WO class 1 — WO class II	WO class 1
1st sergeant — master sergeant	staff sergeant — sergeant
sergeant 1st class — sergeant	
corporal — private 1st class	corporal — lance corporal

72. DEUTSCHES AFRIKA KORPS

SPECIAL FEATURES

DAK Tropical Field Cap
The cap included with this Internationals uniform is exclusive to this issue. The main Set, with all the equipment, included a sand coloured 1935 pattern helmet.

The field cap is made of sand coloured polyurethane with moulded ventilation eyelets, a false flap outline, circular cockade, national socialist eagle (underneath the late issue black plastic sun goggles) and white inverted 'V' Infantry *waffenfarbe*.

Uniform
The feldbluse, or tropical jacket, is cut with an open collar. The two square, pleated breast pockets have pointed flaps fastened with silver spike buttons and the larger hip pockets are of the same design. Note the breast pocket detail in Plate 75.5. There are four spike buttons to the front where three poppers fasten the jacket. The epaulettes are made of stiffened, unhemmed tunic material with a stencilled white border; they fasten with a single spike button. Plate 72.2 gives a full length view of the feldbluse, trousers and standard four eyelet brown ankle boots.

Insignia
The fabric insignia are shown in detail in Plate 72.1. Collar patches have white infantry *waffenfarbe* on a sand coloured backing. On the left sleeve is a brown triangular patch with the single *greifreiter's*, or lance corporals' stripe. Sewn to the right sleeve is a fabric cuff band in sand, white and green with 'Afrika Korps' text. Note the absence of swastika on the eagle badge glued to the right breast.

The white metal belt buckle clasp detail, with an eagle over a circular wreath and central swastika, can be seen in Plate 72.1.

Equipment
The water bottle is attached to the belt by a lug at the top of the bottle. The black polyurethane scabbard is moulded with a point and ball at its tip; a rim around the top fits onto the bayonet frog. Plate 72.4 illustrates the 'Y' straps with the moulded centre ring.

A profile of the KAR98K rifle, with its black polyurethane strap, can be seen in Plate 72.1.

Helmet
The coalscuttle *stehlhelm* issued with the full equipment Set is shown in Plate 72.5. Note the moulded outline of the insignia shield on its right hand side – there were no paper or shield transfers for this piece. The sand coloured scarf can also be seen in this plate.

QUARTERMASTER

- helmet
- goggles
- tunic and trousers
- scarf
- boots
- cartridge belt and Y straps
- water bottle
- bayonet and scabbard
- grenades
- Kar 98k rifle

Separate Equipment Card:
- DAK cap
- tunic and trousers
- boots

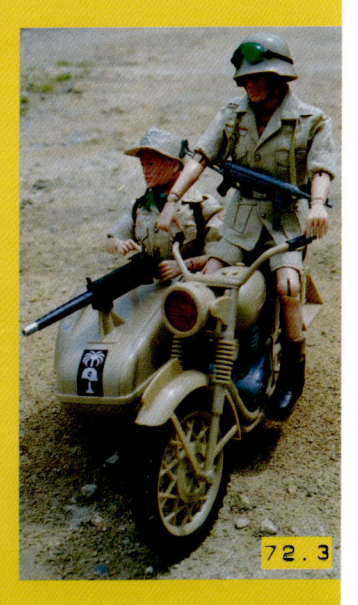

72. DEUTSCHES AFRIKA KORPS

72.1

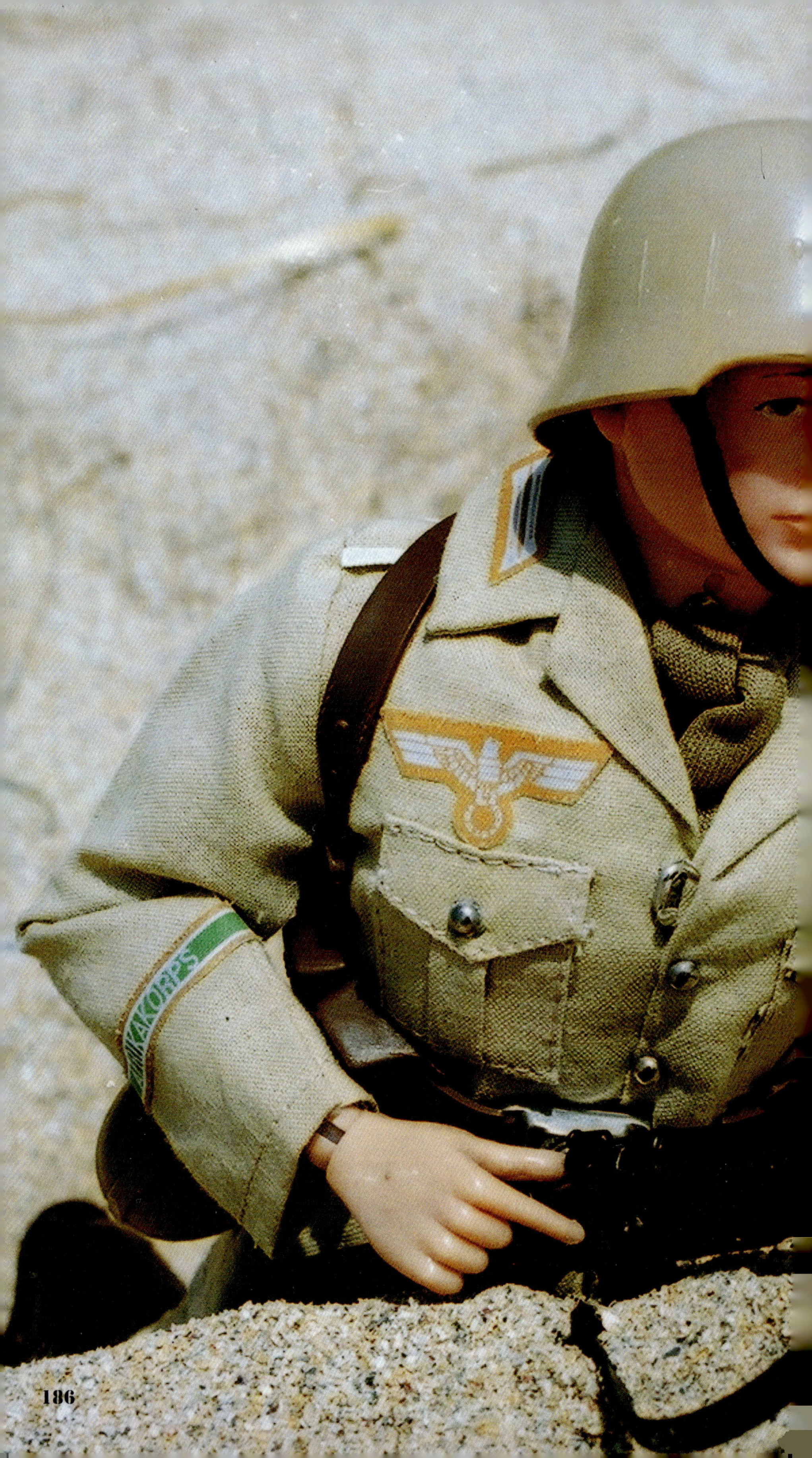

72. DEUTSCHES AFRIKA KORPS

Motorcycle and Sidecar
The Germans used two main types of heavy motorcycle for reconnaissance and communications duties during the War, a BMW and a Zundapp. The Action Man bike is based on neither. Made in hard plastic of four different colours – sand, black, red and metallic grey – it has a black paper rectangular badge on the sidecar depicting a variant of the stencilled Afrika Korps insignia, with palm tree and helmet device in white. The machine gun shown in Plate 72.6 is a late issue version of the standard Browning .30 calibre, moulded in black plastic.

72.6

72.5

73. RUSSIAN INFANTRYMAN

QUARTERMASTER

- helmet
- greatcoat
- trousers
- marching boots

SPECIAL FEATURES

Helmet
This set included the 1940 pattern helmet. Made of dark green plastic, the strap was made from a lighter colour of green moulded polyurethane, which fitted through the two lugs at each side of the helmet. There were arrow shaped tongues at the end of the strap, which could not be adjusted.

Greatcoat
The light grey double-breasted shinel great coat has a wrapover front fastened by three-poppers. The diagonally cut cuffs are large with a single hem and worn folded back as far as the elbow. Only two spike buttons hold the purple-edged, stiffened and unhemmed epaulettes in place. The back is plain with only a centre seam and no half belt at the waist.

Diamond-shaped pre-Babarossa collar tab insignia were used to identify both rank and the arm of service. The plain raspberry colour of the tabs in this instance indicate an infantryman.

Also included in this set are a pair of lime green trousers cut to a jodhpur *sharovari* pattern (similar to the Soldiers of the Century Set in Plate 17.1) and a standard pair of black polyurethane marching boots.

Anti-Tank Grenades
These are the outsized anti-tank grenades issued with the first Soldiers of the Century Set. The metal coloured moulded plastic grenade has a painted steel grey body and a sand-coloured handle. Each grenade has a brass ring looped through a lug at the base.

73.2

73. RUSSIAN INFANTRYMAN

73.1

74. GERMAN PARATROOPER

QUARTERMASTER

- helmet
- greatcoat
- trousers
- marching boots

SPECIAL FEATURES

Helmet
The grey plastic helmet does not have the standard *stahlhelm* wide neck shield. The right side of helmet has a small tricolour national shield; on the left is a paper eagle sticker edged in airforce grey. The black polyurethane chinstrap is the non-adjustable arrow tongue type and is fixed to lugs at both sides of the helmet and at the back. Note the moulded air hole and the identity tag chain.

Smock
The thigh length open collar camouflage smock is made of the Action Man pattern camouflage introduced in the First Issue series. Fastened at the front by three poppers, the separate sleeve cuffs are fastened by a single popper. There are two rounded breast flaps which both have a black fabric tab on the inner edge. Square thigh pockets are open and covered by a rectangular flap. There are no buttons at the smock's front, but there are a series of eight plain spike buttons around the hem of the skirt. A triangular green fabric Luftwaffe eagle is glued to the right breast, just below the pocket flap. Again the swastika in its talons was omitted.

Held in the left hand of the *Fallschimjager* in Plate 74.1 is the dark blue plastic Walther pistol from a late issue weapons Arsenal card.

Trousers and Boots
The plain light grey trousers are made of thin late issue material. Fastened by a single popper, the ankles have white four-cord elastic loops. The boots included in the set are the standard four-eyelet black ankle-length ski boots.

Paratroops in Hitler's Germany formed part of the Luftwaffe instead of being part of army formations, as in Britain and the US. This is why the eagle insignia, seen here on the camouflaged tunic and the cut down para helmet, has the curved wings of the airforce rather than the more angular Wehrmacht version.

74. GERMAN PARATROOPER

74.1

75. US PARATROOPER

QUARTERMASTER

- helmet
- jacket and trousers
- boots
- cartridge belt and straps
- water bottle
- bayonet and scabbard
- rifle

SPECIAL FEATURES

Uniform

The jacket fastens at the neck with one of three front poppers. Separate cuffs are also fastened with poppers, and there is a brass spike button on each unhemmed epaulette and cuff. There are four pockets on the jacket and two thigh pockets on the trousers, each fastened by two spike buttons with stitching across the centre of each pocket. Both pockets and flaps are set diagonally. Knee ties on the trousers are sewn into the inner seam of the legs.

Note the duller finish on this late issue M1 helmet, with straps moulded from sand coloured polyurethane which are not adjustable. The high brown boots, shown in Plate 75.1, are moulded to the basic Action Soldier pattern. The arrow tongue for the sand coloured belt can also be seen in this plate.

Webbing and Equipment

There are sets of four ammunition pouches on each side of the waist, with an individual rectangular first aid dressing pouch moulded on the right side of the Paratrooper's webbing. The canteen cover has no back – instead the canteen is held in place by threading the water bottle's neck through a hole at the top. Beside this is the bayonet frog, which holds the green plastic scabbard for the First Issue pattern bayonet. Note the moulding of the belt and the initials 'US' on the canteen cover. The cross straps of the polyurethane 1941 pattern webbing can be seen in Plate 75.3.

Insignia

The Stars & Stripes badge on the right sleeve was used for recognition when behind enemy lines. It is made of embroidered cloth and sewn onto the tunic. The insignia on the left sleeve is the double 'A' Airborne divisional fabric sticker badge and an oval shaped paras wings badge glued above the left breast pocket.

Detail of the uniform badges and helmet straps can be seen in Plate 75

This Set was based on the World War Two uniform of the US 82nd Airborne Division which was heavily involved in the D-Day and Arnhem operations. The light green two piece uniform is specially adapted for airborne troops, with large pockets and knee ties on the trousers. This is a late issue version of the Set as all the pockets are unhemmed.

75. US PARATROOPER

76. US MARINE

QUARTERMASTER

- helmet
- jacket and trousers
- boots

SPECIAL FEATURES

Uniform
This is based on a plain USMC uniform made of original dungaree material. The open necked jacket has a rounded open pocket on the left breast, four front buttons and a three-popper fastening. The separate cuffs also fasten with a popper each. The USMC globe, anchor and eagle fabric badge is glued to the uniform, as are the rank stripes on each arm.

The trousers have little embellishment other than the two rectangular pocket flaps below the front of the waistband.

Boots issued with this set are in the standard Action Soldier eight-eyelet pattern, but with equal sized mould numbers – 1 and 2 – on the heels. These late issue pairs are shinier than the First Issue versions.

Helmet
The complete corporal's uniform includes a plain polyurethane M1 helmet, not the camouflaged GI Joe one shown in Plate 76.1. By this period the elastic chin straps and brass clips have been replaced by a plain black polyurethane strap held in place by rounded pins on the helmet rim (see Plate 70.1).

194

76. US MARINE

77. HELICOPTER PILOT

QUARTERMASTER

- crash helmet and visor
- flight suit
- boots

There are three different Action Man helicopter pilot sets, all based on the standard pattern one piece zippered suit first introduced with the Action Pilot.

SPECIAL FEATURES

Flight Suit
The green suit illustrated in Plate 77.1 is for the 1st Cavalry (Division) Airmobile, denote by the yellow triangular shield on the left sleeve. There are yellow textured fabric stripes reaching from the arm to the ankles. The rear arm stripes can be seen in Plate 77.2.

Helmet
The Crash Ballistic Protective Flying Helmet is new pattern Action Man piece with a plain bla polyurethane strap. Plate 77.2 shows the larger divisional fabric badge on the back.

This type of helmet includes a transparent green anti-glare visor fitted underneath the visor cover. The visor can be moved up and down through a slit in this cover, which is made of the same plastic as the main helme

77.2

77. HELICOPTER PILOT

77.1

78. UNITED NATIONS SOLDIER

QUARTERMASTER

- beret
- shirt and trousers
- armband
- boots

SPECIAL FEATURES

Uniform
Another simple set from the series, this uniform comprises a short sleeve shirt, plain trousers, beret, armband and standard black ankle boots. The light blue beret is moulded in a late issue circular pattern with a UN beret badge printed on a circular paper sticker.

The trousers and open-necked shirt are of light green material. The shirt has pleated square breast pockets and simple, unhemmed epaulettes fastened by a single button. There is a two-popper fastening, with three buttons to the front and one on each breast pocket. Sleeves are elbow-length with a turn up, shown here just below the armband.

The armband is made of light blue material with 'UN' printed in white letters. It fastens with a single popper.

78.2

78.1

78. UNITED NATIONS SOLDIER

icon
ACTION man®

THE 01

FICERS

PLATES 79-86

79. RAF BATTLE OF BRITAIN PILOT

QUARTERMASTER

- flying helmet
- goggles
- scarf
- jacket and trousers
- belt
- flying boots
- life jacket

SPECIAL FEATURES

Flying Helmet and Goggles
This scrambling member of 'the Few' is an example of the 1940 era RAF officers' blue-grey service dress with the single pilot's rank ribbon band sewn onto the sleeve.

The open-collar tunic has two pleated breast pockets with unhemmed and stiffened scalloped flaps. The cuffs are plain and there are no epaulettes. The two larger square hip pockets have plain rectangular hemmed flaps. Each pocket is fastened with a patterned brass spike button, and there are a further four on the single breast of the tunic. Note the single vent on the back.

Trousers are fastened by a single popper, and the tunic by a further two. The cloth belt and plain square brass buckle can be clearly seen in Plate 79.3.

Over the left breast pocket is a fabric RAF eagle and crown pilot's wings badge and underneath is a blue and white striped medal ribbon for either the Distinguished Flying Medal or Distinguished Flying Cross.

Flying Helmet, Goggles and Scarf
This Action Man Set includes a black polyurethane B-type flying helmet, which has a separate facemask and black ribbed hose in the same pattern as the British Infantryman's. Note the ear guards seen in Plate 79.2, and the moulding on the eight 'stitched' segments of the helmet.

The flying goggles are made from a single mould in clear plastic and fastened with black four-cord elastic. The red nylon scarf is common with the Luftwaffe Pilot Set.

Flying Boots
The new pattern flying boots are also common with the Luftwaffe Pilot Set. These are calf-length, higher than the German Stormtrooper and Russian Infantryman pieces. The shoe is more curved with a full length seam at the back and there is an embossed strap and buckle at the front of the top, under the hem.

Life Jacket
The 'Mae West ' is a canary yellow, cotton life jacket, foam filled at the front and around the neck, with a single turnover hem sewn in yellow cotton. There are three sets of white tapes: a loose top tie, a U-shaped tie in the centre and another single tie at the bottom. All three of the pockets on the left side are shown in Plate 79.1. On the right is a pocket with a stiffened fabric flap fastened by another set of white tape ties. The life jacket is heavily cut away from the shoulders, as seen in Plate 79.2.

79 RAF BATTLE OF BRITAIN PILOT

79.1

80. LUFTWAFFE PILOT

QUARTERMASTER

- flying helmet
- goggles
- scarf
- jacket and trousers
- belt
- Luger pistol and holster
- flying boots
- life jacket

SPECIAL FEATURES

Uniform
The uniform featured in this set is for a Captain, as denoted by the epaulettes, the three wings and oak leaf design on the yellow pilot's collar patches. The grey flying tunic has a grey and white Luftwaffe eagle on the right breast, shown in Plate 80.3. On the lower left side is the eagle and oak leaf pilot's badge. Note the diagonally double sewn pocket outline on the tunic and the white edging on the tunic's collar, which fastens with two poppers. The silver and white epaulettes are fastened by a plain silver spike button and have yellow *waffenfarbe* edging with two printed diamond shaped gold pips, as seen in Plate 80.2. Note the 'V' cut at the wrist of the jacket.

Trousers have a single popper fastening and four-cord elastic foot loops. The broad separately stitched waistband and stiffened unhemmed front pocket flaps can be seen in Plate 80.3. Also shown is the black PVC pistol belt, with its officer's plain silver buckle, the red flying scarf, and the holster for the standard Action Man Luger.

Life Jacket
Plate 80.1 gives a clear view of the embossed buff coloured PVC life jacket. It is fastened by buff herringbone cotton tape threaded through two loops at the base of the vest and tied at the back. There is no rear fastening on the life jacket, unlike the Scramble pattern piece, hence the 'high collar' effect shown here. Also shown are the printed black air valve and centre buckles.

Flying Helmet
The flying helmet has a plain face mask with hose and goggles as illustrated in Plate 80.4. The facemask is fastened by fitting the straps through a hole beneath the moulded buckle on the facemask. The plain plastic goggles are edged with grey paint and connected to the black polyurethane strap by round-headed pins. Plate 80.2 illustrates the moulding detail of the seams and tabs on the flying helmet together with the simple fastening for the lifejacket.

204

80. LUFTWAFFE PILOT

80.1

81. PANZER CAPTAIN

QUARTERMASTER

- cap
- goggles
- scarf
- panzer tunic and trousers
- belt
- trousers
- Luger and holster
- map and case
- binoculars

SPECIAL FEATURES

Jacket and Insignia
An example of the black double breasted tanker's jacket, with a Wehrmacht eagle on the left breast (the laurel leaf circle is left blank with no swastika). The sleeves are plain with a similar 'V' cut sleeve to the Luftwaffe pilot jacket. Two poppers fastened the Panzer captain's tunic on the right side with the left side wrapping across the front of the jacket.

This uniform is provided with a lot of decorations including pink-edged skull and crossbones panzer collar patches and silver and white captain's rank epaulettes with the two gold pips and stylised 'GD' initials. These, and the collar, were edged in pink *waffenfarbe*, denoting the panzer arm. Also shown are the crossed swords and stelhelm of the Silver Wound Badge (awarded for three or four battle wounds), and the gold and black 'Tank Battle' badge (different classes were awarded for various numbers of tank engagements, or the number of continuous days in the field). On the right sleeve is the black and white GrossDeutschland (Greater Germany) fabric cuff band.

Cap and Goggles
The light grey officer's peaked cap is moulded from single piece of polyurethane and adorned by a silver eagle, moulded silver cords and a black peak. The goggles are non-standard, the actual set include a late issue polyurethane strap piece and similar late issue binoculars (again later Action Man standard issue with hollow eye pieces and a polyurethane strap, rather than the single-cord elastic).

Trousers, Scarf and Belt
The plain black trousers have two thigh pockets with stiffened flaps on the trousers. These flaps are curved with a central semi-circle in the middle representing the button tabs. They are fastened by a single popper and also have white four-cord elastic foot loops. Standard black ankle length boots were included with the set.

Also shown in Plate 81.1 are the plain light grey scarf and the belt buckle attached to a much thinner black PVC pebble-effect belt.

81.2

81. PANZER CAPTAIN

81.1

82. CAMP KOMMANDANT

QUARTERMASTER

- cap
- greatcoat
- shirt
- belt
- trousers
- Luger and holster
- swagger stick

SPECIAL FEATURES

Greatcoat
Part of the Colditz series, this German officer is dressed in a double breasted *feld grau* greatcoat fastened with three poppers and featuring four double rows of golden spike buttons. Made of a similar material to its British and French counterparts (see Plates 57 and 83) this piece has hemmed and folded cuffs, two slanted pocket flaps and plain, stiffened fabric epaulettes. A rear view of the greatcoat in Plate 82.2 shows the half-belt, which has three golden spike buttons, the centre back seam above and single vent below.

A plain shirt is worn underneath the greatcoat (see Plate 82.3). Fastened by two poppers, it has two simplified red and white *waffenfarbe* patches on the collar. The Kommandant Set also includes standard black marching boots (see Plate 16.2), plain grey green trousers and the swagger stick first issued in the Army Officer Set (see Plate 54.2).

Cap
Clearly shown in Plate 82.3 is the detail at the front of the moulded polyurethane officer's cap – the national eagle emblem, and an oakleaf cluster with a red, white and black cockade in its centre. Moulded cords are painted silver and the cap band and peak are painted black.

Mauser
The Model 1916 Mauser Automatic Pistol was first introduced by the Germans in 1895. The original weapon held an eight 9mm round magazine, but was largely obsolete by the start of the Second World War as the smaller Lugers, or Walthers were more practical.

The Action Man Mauser shown in Plate 82.3 is part of the Small Arms/Armoury series and is made from a single mould of dark blue plastic with a red-brown painted grip. Plate 82.3 provides a close-up of this piece and some detail of the texture of the belt and holster

82. CAMP KOMMANDANT

82.1

83. ESCAPE OFFICER

QUARTERMASTER

- cap
- wool hat
- greatcoat
- scarf
- trousers
- boots ID tag
- compass
- torch
- mug
- Luger revolver
- rope
- suitcase

SPECIAL FEATURES

Greatcoat
A member of the 17th/21st Lancers, as can be seen from the cap insignia, the escape officer wears a khaki British greatcoat. Plate 83.1 clearly illustrates the slanted hip pocket flap, the gold spike buttons and the size of the collar. The thickness of the weave on the material can also be seen. A rear view in Plate 83.2 details the centre back seam, epaulettes and half belt, with the three brass spike buttons.

The peaked cap is the same as the one issued with the British Army Officer Set (see Plate 54.1). A knitted green balaclava helmet is also included in the set and can be seen in Plate 82.3. The weapon being held here by the escapee in Plate 83.1 is a .38 Colt Special, also included in the Small Arms/Armoury series.

Case
The ivy green plastic escape suitcase is made from two half moulds and snapped together. Plate 83.3 shows the interior of the case and the torch (based on the same pattern as the piece issued with the original Crash Crew Set, see Plate 25.2).

Inside the suitcase, the Escape Officer has at his disposal a white plastic tape recorder, linked by a single cord of white elastic to a microphone, a standard Luger with a red-brown shoulder stock which fits around the outline of the pistol grip and a long black silencer to fit over the Luger's barrel.

83. ESCAPE OFFICER

83.1

84. BRITISH ARMY MAJOR

QUARTERMASTER

- cap
- tunic and trousers
- pistol belt
- colt .45 and holster
- boots
- map and case
- binoculars

Special Operations Tent:
- tent
- base
- pegs poles and guy ropes
- folding table
- folding stool

SPECIAL FEATURES

Uniform
Based on the style of the British Infantryman's jacket, the insignia on the left arm is for the same unit (see Plate 19.1). Both tunic and trousers are made from a thinner and lighter material, similar to that used for the Dispatch Rider Set in Plate 56.1. The plain cut trousers are a new design, with two pointed rear pocket flaps and a silver metal rivet and stud button popper. Also issued with this uniform was the standard peak cap with a new metal insignia: 'ER' initials at the centre of the laurel and crown, see Plate 84.1.

Note the texture of the uniform and the stitching on the breast pockets, also the neck cord for the pistol – a late issue Colt .45 with a moulded rectangular lug at the base of the grip – and the late issue light grey map case with smaller black lettering.

Special Operations Tent
The Special Operations Tent is a far simpler affair than either its Explorer or Pup Tent predecessors. There are four small posts in each corner of the canvas, which fit into slots in the hollow plastic rectangular base. In the centre are two longer poles, which connect to a ridgepole. The canvas is anchored with guy ropes fitted over the tip of the corner poles and slipped onto moulded plastic hooks in the base. The centre of the base is filled by a rectangular sheet of green cardboard, large enough to accommodate the ubiquitous bunk bed.

Pegs on either side of the centre pole can be clearly seen in Plate 84.2, as can a moulded green plastic shovel. This shovel was issued with the Armoured Jeep and is based on the pattern of the Combat Engineer piece (Plate 30.1). This plate also shows some detail of the swagger stick, standard map and green plastic folding table.

84. BRITISH ARMY MAJOR

84.1

85. LATE ISSUE BRITISH ARMY MAJOR

QUARTERMASTER

- cap
- tunic and trousers
- pistol belt
- colt .45 and holster
- boots
- map and case
- binoculars

SPECIAL FEATURES

Uniform
The poorer quality of this later issue version can be easily seen when compared to the previous set of plates. Stiffened, unhemmed fabric on the pocket flaps and 'stitched' pleats in the breast pockets are the most significant changes.

Plate 85.2 shows some detail of the elasticated ankles on the trousers, and the simple unhemmed open pocket on the right thigh. Note the lack of darts in the tunic. On the left thigh of the trousers in Plate 85.3 is the stitched outline of another pocket, similar to the same pattern on the First Issue British Infantryman's. However this version does not have even an outline of a pocket flap.

Insignia
The use of fabric unit, rank and medal ribbons is another development. Plate 85.3 provides a close up view of the unit badges, notably the curved unit title in black at the top of the tunic's arm – 17/21 Lancers and the triangular unit insignia of a black bull on a yellow background. On the epaulettes are fabric crowns which denote a major's rank. A double row medal ribbon is also shown. The service cap has the 'Death o Glory' Lancer badge on a red hatband.

214

85. LATE ISSUE BRITISH ARMY MAJOR

85.1

86. SAS OFFICER

QUARTERMASTER

- cap
- scarf
- jumper
- camouflage trousers
- pistol belt
- Colt .45 and holster
- boots

SPECIAL FEATURES

Uniform
One of the first uniforms in the Special Air Service series, this uniform is nearest to the type of gear worn by the original SAS units, which were formed in 1941 as raiding squads against the Germans and Italians in the North Africa.

The single popper camouflage trousers are an unlikely feature. This Action Man Set includes a variant of the original pattern first introduced in the Beachhead Assault Set (see Plate 7.1). The trousers included in this uniform set have a deep rectangular left thigh pocket with a pointed pocket flap.

The ribbed khaki jumper is made from a nylon material cut to a V-neck pattern. It has a separately stitched waist band and plain unhemmed epaulettes. Also seen in Plate 86.2 is the sand coloured scarf, distinct in colour from the green or brown versions issued with previous Paratroop regiment uniforms.

Cap
The standard British Officer's brown peaked service cap has an outsized winged dagger emblem in silver coated plastic with the unit motto 'Who Dares Wins', as seen in Plate 86.2.

86.2

86. SAS OFFICER

THE SPECI

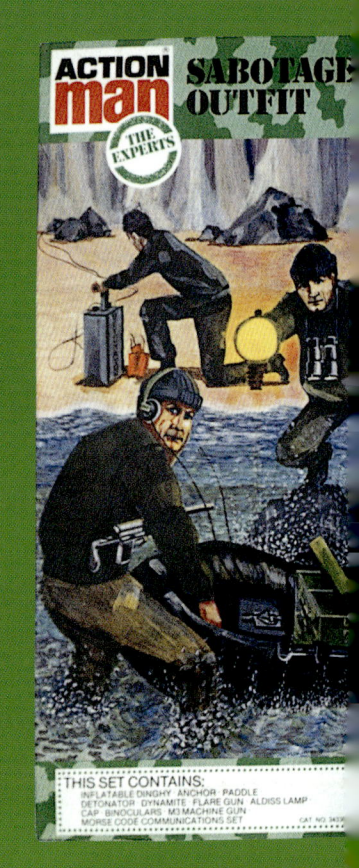

LISTS

PLATES 87-95

87. COMMANDO

QUARTERMASTER

- cap
- jacket and trousers
- boots
- ammunition bandoliers
- M60 machine gun
- face camouflage crayons

SPECIAL FEATURES

Uniform

A modern raider designated by the inclusion of the M60 machine gun, Plate 87.1 is a full view of the zippered plain green uniform with its crossed black rubber bullet belts. This plate shows the different styles on the pockets – large square pleated hip ones, and simple angled breast pockets, both of which have plain rectangular flaps.

The uniform included in this set is plain in its design – simple pattern trousers with one popper and no pockets. The open jacket is fastened by a silver YKK zip and has plain sleeve cuffs, and no epaulettes. The black rubber version of the knitted cap is also included. Note the detail of the ribbing on the hat in Plate 87.2. Standard black ankle boots complete the uniform.

M60 Machine Gun and Ammunition

A close up of the M60 is seen in Plate 87.2. The ammunition belts are held together by two rubber pins on the underside of the bullets and are based on a similar pattern mould to the silver polyurethane versions. There are no mould numbers or inscriptions on either piece.

87. COMMANDO

87.1

88. ROYAL ENGINEERS

QUARTERMASTER

- helmet
- battle dress tunic and trousers
- ammunition boots
- belt and pouches
- canteen
- dagger and scabbard
- Lee Enfield rifle
- mine detector

An example of a uniform available in the new 'book style' packaging, first issued in 1975. This set includes the standard late issue British uniform with elasticated ankles, simpler pockets and a variant of the sand coloured 1937 pattern webbing.

Also included, but not shown here is a late variant of the mine detector. This has similar head and pole pieces to those used in the First Issue set (see Plates 23.1, and 23.2). But these only connect to a pair of the green and black headphones (originally included in the French Resistance Fighter's set, see Plate 18.1), with no US style backpack.

SPECIAL FEATURES

Webbing
The rear view in Plate 88.2 gives some detail of the webbing, with moulded straps for the green plastic water bottle – based on an original piece included in British Infantryman's Set in the Soldier's of the Century Series. Note the angled strap at the top of the bottle, and the T-shaped tongue and buckle at the base. The webbing for this Set does not include the entrenching tool pouch on the left hip which is cut from the full mould (cut marks can be seen). Note the moulded detail on the webbing in Plate 88.3.

This version of the dagger and scabbard is also included in the Long Range Desert Group Set which follows.

Lee Enfield Rifle
Also shown in Plate 88.3 is the bolt operated .303 SMLE rifle (Short Magazine Lee Enfield), No. 4 Mk 1 with a 10 round magazine. Whilst the Lee Enfield was the standard British rifle used throughout World War Two this is the 1944 version which replaced the short barrelled No.1 Mk 3 weapon universally used in the opening campaigns in France and North Africa. The Action Man piece is made of brown plastic with spray painted black metal parts along the barrel and magazine. The late issue black polyurethane strap and moulded strap pins on the rifle are clearly shown.

Insignia
The detail of the red and blue shoulder flash with the Engineers' regimental title can clearly be seen on the arm of the jacket in Plate 88.3.

88. ROYAL ENGINEERS

88.1

89. LONG RANGE DESERT ROUP

QUARTERMASTER

- headdress and head band
- scarf
- shirt
- shorts
- socks
- boots
- belt and pouches
- entrenching tool
- dagger and scabbard
- Thompson Sub Machine Gun

Separate Armoury Card:
- Lewis gun
- magazine
- bipod

SPECIAL FEATURES

Uniform
The Long Range Desert Group was formed in 1941 to compliment the original SAS units. Plate 89.1 is a full length view of the uniform. The simple sand coloured shorts have a separately sewn waistband and fasten with a single popper (see Plate 89.3). The shirt is made of a similar material; it is based on the short-sleeved shirt pattern included with the Internationals' United Nations Soldier Set (see Plate 78.2) with three sand coloured buttons and a pleated breast pocket with scalloped flap. Note the blue fabric winged parachute badge over the left breast pocket and the sand and white fabric corporal's chevrons on the sleeves.

Standard brown ankle length boots are worn with sand coloured ribbed nylon calf-length socks. These are based on the same pattern as the footballer's and feature the reversed stitching on the seams (see Plate 36.1).

Thompson Submachine Gun
This Trooper is armed with a new Action Man weapon, the 0.45 calibre 1928A1 Thompson Submachine Gun, with an early type fore grip and muzzle compensator.

The original weapon was fitted with a 20 round box magazine, although 50 round drum magazines were also used by the British under US Lend Lease agreements.

The Action Man piece is moulded in dark blue plastic with red-brown painted butt and grips. The black polyurethane strap loops around the pin on the butt and the fore grip. 'Made in Hong Kong' is embossed on the butt in capitals. Also shown the sand coloured polyurethane 1937 pattern webbing with large rectangular ammunition pouches.

Headdress
The white native-style head scarf is made from a single piece of white cotton, with a large dart at the back, and is held in place by a loop of chestnut coloured six-cord elastic. There is also a simple triangular brown cotton neck scarf (see Plate 89.3).

Equipment
The entrenching tool pouch can be seen in Plate 89.2. It is of the same pattern as the piece included in the Australian Jungle Fighter Set (see Plate 20.1). The head of the entrenching tool fits into the mould of the folding pouch halves, with the shaft, used as a pin, fitting into the two moulded lugs to keep the pouch closed.

Plate 89.3 shows the silver polyurethane commando-style throwing dagger and its plastic chestnut brown sheath, which fits through a moulded frog above the entrenching tool. Note the moulding webbing detail and belt clip.

Lewis Gun
The Trooper in Plate 89.3 is manning a Mark 1 Lewis Machine Gun, moulded in dark blue plastic with separate brown plastic butt and pistol grip parts. The serrated circular drum magazine is a separate piece, fixed to a pin at the top of the main body of the weapon. A, by now standard, black polyurethane strap is fitted to two pins on the butt and barrel. There are no markings or inscriptions on this piece.

89. LONG RANGE DESERT GROUP

90. SAS COMMANDER

QUARTERMASTER

- smoke hood
- gas mask
- boiler suit
- boots
- flak jacket
- belt and ammunition pouch
- Colt .45 and holster
- Heckler & Koch MP5

Prior to the storming of the Iranian Embassy in 1980, little if anything was known about the modern SAS and its methods as all official covert operations were just that.

SPECIAL FEATURES

Uniform
Plate 90.1 shows the SAS Commander uniform that is the basic uniform used for the SAS series. Based on a black one-piece boiler suit, it has black twelve-cord elastic cuffs and ankles and is elasticated at the back of the waist. Note the left thigh pocket with its simple rectangular flap made from stiffened cotton fabric. The suit is fastened by two poppers and has a simple stand collar.

Flak Vest
The First Issue pattern of black flak vest is illustrated here. Made from a single piece, the embossed PVC is heat sealed over thin foam to provide body and give the impression of bulk. Fitting over the head, the vest fastens with four T-shaped tongues, two on each side of the waist. These slot into slits on the front of the vest (see the end of the 'T' under the right elbow of the Trooper in Plate 90.1) The embossed front flap and right pocket can also be seen.

Late Issue versions are made of thicker criss-crossed PVC with no chest detail and are fastened by two sets of silver rivet button poppers on each side of the waist.

Belt and Weapons
The SAS Commander uniform was issued with a simple black cotton belt, with three rows of stitching and First Issue pattern brass fasteners. Attached to the belt is a set of four black polyurethane ammunition pouches, standard Action Man grenades, and a black pistol holster with a brass circular rivet. However no PVC thigh strap was included. In the holster is a black plastic version of the Colt M1911 A1 .45.

The weapon issued with this basic SAS Trooper Set is the Heckler & Koch MP5, a standard weapon in counter terrorist units and modern specialist forces. Small and compact with a 30 round curved magazine of 9mm bullets this version of the MP5 has its collapsible stock extended. The Action Man piece does not have any markings or inscriptions.

Gas Mask and Smoke Hood
Close-up detail of the gas mask and smoke hood can be seen in Plate 90.2. The smoke hood is made from two pieces of grey cotton sewn together with a single seam running from the back and over the crown. At the front is an elasticated circle which fits over the S6 gas mask. The mask itself is made from a single piece of black plastic and has two eyeholes that are glazed by one piece of transparent plastic glued to the inside of the mask. Note the moulded contours for the nose, and filters on the left and over the mouth.

90. SAS COMMANDER

91. SAS SECRET MISSION POD & ASSAULT CRAFT

QUARTERMASTER

- pod
- inflatable dingy
- oar
- sea anchor
- flare gun
- Bren gun and bipod
- pulley

Assault Craft
- outboard motor
- cover
- paddles
- life vest
- rope
- demolition harness
- knives and scabbards
- entrenching tool
- detonator
- wire roll
- dynamite
- EM2 rifle and scope

SPECIAL FEATURES

Life Vest and EM2
Using the standard Commander's uniform, the Trooper shown in Plate 91.1 is wearing an all black PVC life vest from the Assault Craft Set. This is based on the original pattern piece included in the Action Pilot's Survival Set (see Plate 14.1. A rear view of the life vest can be seen in Plate 91.2. The set also includes a late issue Saboteur's knitted cap.

The set includes a new weapon based on the British EM2 (Experimental Model).

Designed in a similar configuration to the current smaller SA80 rifle used by the British armed forces, the EM2 has the magazine behind the pistol grip. A 7mm calibre rifle, it was developed by the British in 1952 but was not subsequently introduced since the SLR was adopted in preference as this used standardised 7.62mm NATO ammunition (see Plate 43.3).

The Action Man piece is moulded from a single piece of black plastic, with no markings or inscriptions. The main polyurethane rifle strap is connected to two pins on the barrel and butt. A circular black night sight is fixed to a 'T' bracket at the top of the rifle, and has separate transparent red lens caps at both ends of the sight. The sight is fitted with a polyurethane strap (see Plate 91.3).

SAS Secret Mission Pod
Shown in Plate 91.1 is the black plastic cylindrical mission pod itself. This is moulded in two halves, held together by two yellow polyurethane collars which twist around grooves moulded into the end of each half. The collars are connected by standard yellow rope. Prominent yellow SAS initials and black and yellow stripes can also be seen here.

In the background is the black PVC tent from the Assault Craft. The rubber dinghy is moulded to the same pattern as the original green version shown in Plate 110.1. The tent, which was only included in this set, is fixed to the base of the boat and fastened by two sets of poppers. The inside is moulded in orange PVC and there are two clear panels on each side of the folded covering.

Also included in the Secret Mission Pod is a standard pattern black PVC Life Raft (see Plate 29.1) and a black plastic pulley and hook. The pulley is decorated with a yellow and black SAS insignia sticker.

Ammunition Belt
The four pouch ammunition belt has a Hasbro ® Hong Kong inscription on the back. The pouches do not have folded or opening flaps unlike the First Issue pieces. Note the black pistol butt and the soft metal '8' shaped connecting loop in Plate 91.2.

Secret Mission Harness
The Secret Mission harness in Plate 91.3 fits around the waist with a, now standard, T-shaped tongue and rectangular buckle. The chest-high shoulder straps slot into each side of the back black polyurethane harness, and can be adjusted. Incongruously there are also slots on each shoulder for the standard polyurethane bayonet and scabbard (see Plate 43.4), and a moulded pouch on the right chest strap. Note the black demolition wireroll with silver, instead of copper, wire. There is a Hasbro ® inscription on one of the sides of the wireroll.

Demolition Harness
The demolition harness again uses pieces from previous sets, in this case a black detonator from the Saboteur Set and the dynamite (see Plates 11.2 and 29.2). These are held in place by a black elastic band which fits around the harness before it is fitted on to the Action Man figure. As well as the moulded water bottle cover on the right hip, there is a bayonet frog on the left and a lug in the centre of the back Plate 91.3 gives a back view of this harness.

NOT SHOWN: the entrenching tool (an all black version of the Australian Jungle Fighter's entrenching tool with black head, hilt and PVC loop).

91. SAS SECRET MISSION POD & ASSAULT CRAFT

91.1

92. SAS FROGMAN

QUARTERMASTER

- headpiece
- top
- trousers
- facemask
- flippers
- assault vest
- belt
- diver's depth gauge
- air cylinders
- knife and scabbard
- dynamite
- grappling hook
- wire cutters
- Heckler & Koch

SPECIAL FEATURES

Equipment

Around the waist, the standard pattern SAS black cotton belt threads through loops on the vest and fastens at the back. The ammunition pouch is positioned on the right hip, and on the left hip is the bolt cutter holder (a square of black PVC with two slits at the top which fits through the belt, with two holes below through which slide the arms of the bolt cutter). The bolt cutters themselves are made from black plastic with yellow painted handles; a Made in Hong Kong inscription appears on one of the arms. Plate 92.2 shows some detail of the bolt cutter holder.

At the feet of the Frogman in Plate 92.1 is the black polyurethane grappling hook with its standard Action Man rope. There are two holes on each side of the vest through which slides one of the prongs of the grappling hook. New pattern flippers have ribbed blades and cut away heels on the moulded shoes. These allow the flippers to be strapped to the belt with a black polyurethane strap. There are no inscriptions or markings on the flippers.

The fixed stock version of the Heckler & Koch MP5 is included in the Set. This piece is moulded with a textured, rather than plain, grip and has a Made in Hong Kong inscription on the butt. The diver's knife has a gloss yellow hilt and is based on an original First Issue piece (see Plate 11.1), but with a blunt end and thicker blade. However the scabbard is different – a rectangular black plastic box with two lugs at the end, through which is threaded a loop of elastic.

Note the YKK inscription on the zipper of the suit, and the detail of the standard diver's watch in Plate 92.3.

Oxygen Tanks

The black oxygen tanks are a copy of the First Issue Underwater Demolition Set piece, with separately moulded cylinders, silver air valve and a black plastic baseplate with Hasbro ® inscription. Plate 92.2 shows some detail of the tanks and the brass grip on the face mask's black six-cord elastic strap.

Assault Vest

Plate 92.3 illustrates the black PVC assault vest, which has a sandwiched layer of thin foam for padding. The vest fits over the neck of the wearer with a semi-circular loop, and is held in place around the waist by the cotton belt. Three vertical pouches are moulded into the vest, the top flap of which can be seen here. Also shown is the black and yellow SAS sticker badge over the bottom of the vest and the yellow hilt of the diver's knife.

The SAS Frogman Set includes the original pattern rubber tunic, trousers and headpiece from the First Issue Navy Frogman Set (see Plate 11). However new items included are a black facemask, a set of black oxygen cylinders, and different style flippers. Plate 92.1 is a full length view of the SAS Frogman.

92. SAS FROGMAN

92.1

93. SAS PARATROOPER

QUARTERMASTER

- crash helmet, visor and facemask
- boiler suit
- parachute harness
- pouch
- bayonet and scabbard
- M-16 Rifle

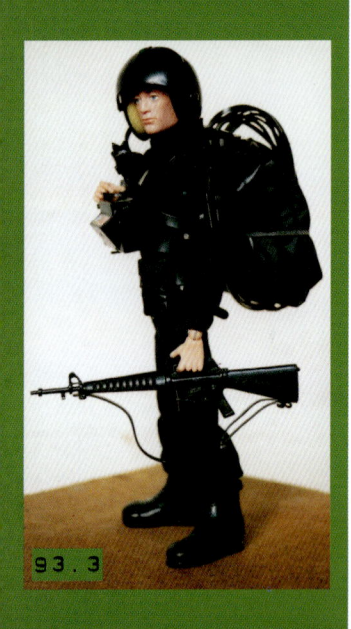

SPECIAL FEATURES

Parachute and Webbing
The descent of this trooper on his black PVC parachute is shown in Plate 93.1. The chute is connected to a plastic backplate by two sets of four PVC straps. The bulk of the folded parachute is held in place by a black elastic strap, one of the foam pads on the inside of the helmet, and the rectangular arm pouch, as shown in Plate 93.3.

The black polyurethane paratrooper's webbing is based on the same piece in the Secret Mission Set, although there are now two additional shoulder strapped pouches and a rectangular ammunition pouch (shown here on the left hip) which is fitted to the belt. In addition to the webbing there is an additional parachute harness and oxygen control box. Plate 93.4 is a rear view of the webbing. Note the chest straps fixed under the left arm. Also shown here is the arrangement for the arm pouch, and the triangular shoulder connector strapped around the arm. An alternative position for the bayonet and scabbard is shown, with the rectangular lug on the right shoulder providing an optional home for the scabbard. The ridged cap of the late issue polyurethane water bottle can also be seen in this plate, as can the discarded parachute harness which illustrates how the PVC 'T' flaps fit into the black plastic harness. All the PVC parachute straps are glued to the harness plate, which does not have any inscription or markings.

The black plastic helmet is based on the same pattern as the Crash Ballistic Protective Flying Helmet included in the Helicopter Pilot Set (see Plate 77.2). Plate 93.2 shows the black and yellow SAS badge and motto sticker on the back. Note the texture of the late issue material on the boiler suit in plate 93.1.

Control Unit
The sticker dials on the top of the oxygen control unit can be seen in Plate 93.2. The pins on either side of the box's top connect to two clear polyurethane tubes (not shown). The right connects to the facemask on the helmet and the left to another pin on the left of the backplate.

M-16 rifle
The late issue M16 seen in Plate 93.3 is moulded with a different pattern of indented barrel grips (contrast this to the First Issue piece in Plate 21.1). The inscription on the butt has been erased and a blank patch left in the moulded wood grain. The loop ring on the pistol grip was also removed from this piece.

93.2

93.3

(The author would like to acknowledge the assistance of the Taylor family in the making of Plate 93.1)

93.4

232

93. SAS PARATROOPER

93.1

94. FIREMAN

There were two main issues for the Fireman's Set in the Emergency series.

SPECIAL FEATURES

First Issue
The first issue, with black PVC waterproof jacket, is shown in Plate 94.1. A simple piece with plain cuffs and no epaulettes or decoration, the jacket is fastened with three poppers and has two plain rectangular pocket flaps on each hip. Also part of the set are the same striped navy blue trousers that were included in the Grenadier Guardsman Set (see Plate 43.1) and the three-quarter length boots issued with the German Stormtrooper Set. The 5" Fireman's axe has a chestnut plastic shaft glued to the red plastic head (there are no markings or inscriptions on this piece). This plate also provides some good detail of the black PVC belt that is based on the original pattern piece from the Crash Crew Set (see Plate 25.1). Note the silver plastic strapcutter in the left hip pouch. Plate 94.2 provides a rear view of the uniform, showing the golden polyurethane pliers and red angle-head torch.

The profile of the yellow plastic helmet is based on a British design (the French Action Group Joe Set included a similar piece in chromed plastic). The crest includes a crown, chevrons, foliage and a flame symbol at the top. Note the First Issue pattern buckle fastening, plus the head of the axe with its part silver painted blade.

Second Issue
An example of the second issue is shown in Plate 94.3. The nylon style jacket and trousers are in a stronger blue and of thinner material than its First Issue counterpart. Whilst the red stripe is still made of the same material, this piece features sewn ridged creases at the front and back of the leg in a similar style to the trousers from the Cricketer Set. This plate also includes the smaller red plastic fire extinguisher (Hasbro ® Hong Kong inscription on the base) with the golden polyurethane head. The haft of the small red plastic fire axe, again based on the same pattern as the Crash Crew piece, can also be seen.

The Fireman's backpack shown in Plate 94.4 can be filled with water via a clear polyurethane plug on the top left of the pack. On the top right is the black plastic pump. By pressing this up and down the water is forced down the black PVC tube and out of a red plastic nozzle clipped on to the left hand side of the pack. Note the simple late issue type of black polyurethane helmet strap, which fits over the pins on either side of the helmet's rim.

QUARTERMASTER

- helmet
- jacket
- trousers
- boots
- belt
- torch
- pliers
- strap cutter
- hand axe
- axe
- fire extinguisher

Separate Equipment Card
- backpack

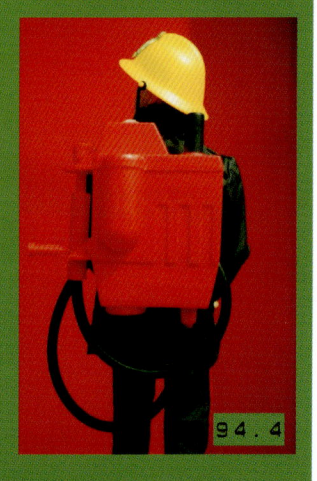

94. FIREMAN

94.1

95. POLICE PATROLMAN

QUARTERMASTER

- crash helmet
- jacket and trousers
- motorcycle boots
- reflective Sam Browne belt
- traffic cones

SPECIAL FEATURES

Helmet
The helmet is based on the original First Issue Scramble Pilot pattern, with the same black polyurethane strap and plastic visor arrangement. However this piece has a blue and white chequered paper sticker strip and a 'POLICE' legend.

Boots
The set shown in Plate 95.1 features a new pattern of calf length boot, with moulded pads on the toes and a zipped rear seam, with straps, at the top of the calf.

Uniform
The uniform itself is a simple one. A jacket in thin black cotton has plain silver spike buttons – four on the front, one on each epaulette and one on each of the scalloped pocket flaps. It fastens at the front with two poppers. The two breast pockets are pleated and hemmed, but the hip pockets just have flaps. The cut of the jacket is open with a silver 'EIIR' crest on each collar point, similar to those included in the Royal Military Police Set (see Plate 55.3)

The trousers are cut in a jodhpur style and have no pockets. Fastening with a single popper this piece also includes black four-cord elastic foot loops. Completing the set is a bright orange 'Sam Browne' style belt and shoulder strap. Simply hemmed and with a square brass buckle, the strap fits over the right shoulder of the wearer.

Plate 95.2 is a rear view of the uniform. Note the centre back seam and waist vent on the jacket, the detail of the boots and the single chequered helmet strip.

NOT SHOWN – orange plastic traffic cones (see Plate 114.1).

236

95. POLICE PATROLMAN

MACHINE GUN AND TRIPOD

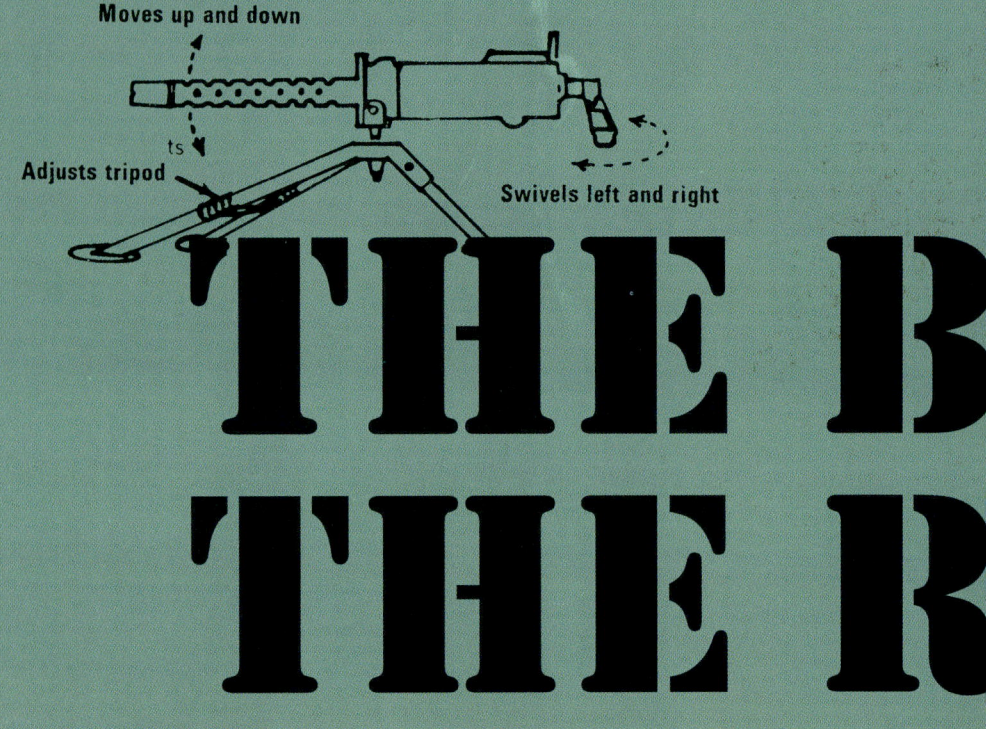

Moves up and down

ts

Adjusts tripod

Swivels left and right

THE B
THE R

MILITARY VEHICLES

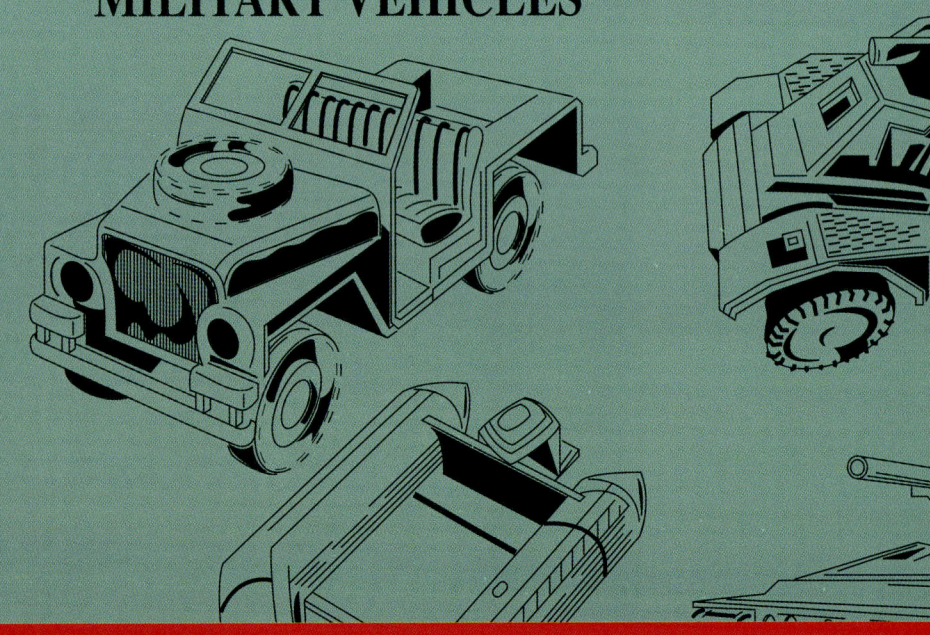

238

REST OF TEST

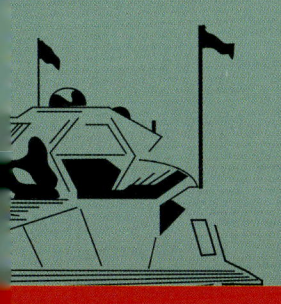

PLATES 96-115

96. SAILOR

QUARTERMASTER

- cap
- vestjacket
- collar
- trousers
- boots

SPECIAL FEATURES

Uniform
This uniform is based on the traditional 'square rig' uniform of the Royal Navy, first introduced in the 19th Century. The basic British sailors' uniform comprises navy blue bell bottomed trousers and a jacket with a square cut collar. This version of the jacket is fastened with two front poppers.

A later issue zip-fastened uniform, with an unhemmed navy collar, was issued in the Frontliners series (Plate 96.3). Note the cuffs on the jacket and the zip with logo and black cotton ribbon.

Underneath the jacket is the simple unhemmed short sleeved white shirt with its blue edging.

Cap
The round white polyurethane cap has a black fabric cap band with the ship's name on it in gold – in this instance HMS Fearless. Other vessels named include HMS Ark Royal, Dreadnought, Raleigh and Victory. The fabric of the hatband and the blue painted rim on the Dreadnought cap can be clearly seen in Plate 96.3. Note the moulded stitching above the cap band and the two air holes at the side.

Collar
The navy collar has three white stripes. A separate piece, it must be tied to the wearer's chest using cotton tapes underneath the jacket. The rear view in Plate 96.2 shows the collar in detail. Note the jacket flap that fits underneath the collar.

A black nylon loop fits over the jacket but underneath the collar.

96. SAILOR

96.1

97. RAF WORKING DRESS

QUARTERMASTER

- cap
- vestjacket
- collar
- trousers
- boots

SPECIAL FEATURES

Uniform
This simple uniform consists of a forage cap, air force grey V neck jumper, greatcoat, coloured belt, trousers and black ankle boots. The grey forage cap is made of a single piece of moulded polyurethane with a gold RAF crest badge on the left side. The grey jumper is made in a woolly textured fabric with no cuffs and simple unhemmed epaulettes. The trousers are also of simple design, with no pockets and fastened by a single popper. Note the late issue ankle boots with the thicker eyelet rings and soles.

Greatcoat and Belt
The greatcoat, whilst based on the standard double breasted Action Man pattern seen in Plate 57.1, is made of a thinner material. The design has been simplified with, for example, no buttons on the cuffs, epaulettes or half belt (see Plate 97.2).

The close up view in Plate 97.3 shows the high collar and double row of four golden spike buttons. Also clearly shown is the elastic fabric on the red, light blue and navy blue coloured belt, connected to a standard pattern buckle.

97.2

97.3

242

97. RAF WORKING DRESS

97.1

98. FIELD TRAINING EXCERCISE

SPECIAL FEATURES

This Set includes a dark green version of the standard one-piece boiler suit with elasticised cuffs and half waist. Also included is the black Royal Tank Regiment beret.

The standard black boots and SLR rifle shown here are all from previous issues.

Walkie-talkie
The walkie-talkie included in this Set can be seen in Plate 98.1. It is made of three different types of plastic and includes an extendible aerial. There are no inscriptions or markings on this piece

QUARTERMASTER

- beret
- overalls
- walkie talkie

99. TOM STONE UNIFORM

SPECIAL FEATURES

Another variant of the standard two-piece camouflage uniform, this still retains the open collar but is significantly different with no buttons, a different shade and colour mix on the USMC camouflage print and only a square breast pocket on the left.

Also included is a green beret with a Parachute Regiment wings badge and a fixed-stock version of the Heckler & Koch MP5 moulded in dark blue plastic with a painted red-brown butt.

100. BRITISH INFANTRYMAN

QUARTERMASTER

- camouflaged helmet
- camouflaged jacket and trousers
- belt and pouches
- pouches
- boots
- Carl Gustav rocket launcher
- bipod

SPECIAL FEATURES

Carl Gustav Rocket Launcher
The Carl Gustav 84mm recoilless rocket launcher fetured in this set was developed by the Swedish firm FFV and is shown in Plate 100.1. It is made from green plastic with a separate sight stuck on the left of the barrel. There is also a moulded plastic bi-pod fixed to the bottom of the weapon.

Uniform
Made from the same material as the Fallschirmjager's smock in Plate 74.1, the DPM (Disruptive Pattern Material) combat jacket in this Set has four rectangular pockets with stiffened but unhemmed pointed pocket flaps. Three poppers fasten the jacket and there were a further two on the separately stitched cuffs. The epaulettes are made of a similar stiffened material as the pocket flaps and are fastened by a gold spike button – the only buttons on the jacket).

The trousers are plain with a single popper at the waist and a thigh pocket on each trouser leg. Note the pointed flap on the left leg, seen in Plate 100.2. Also included are a pair of standard black ankle boots.

Helmet and Webbing
The 1944 pattern helmet has a deeper silhouette than its 1916 pattern predecessor. Moulded with foliage and netting, it is one of the last helmets to include a four-cord elastic strap with rectangular lugs and a brass clip. The only inscription is the mould number under the crown.

The rear view of Plate 100.2 provides a clear view of the kidney pouches on the 1958 pattern green polyurethane webbing.

100. BRITISH INFANTRYMAN

100.1

101. US MACHINE GUNNER

QUARTERMASTER

- helmet
- scarf
- jacket and trousers
- boots
- belt and pouches
- canteen
- bayonet and scabbard
- Browning .30 calibre machine gun
- tripod
- ammunition box
- grenade

This US Machine Gunner is a member of the 3rd Infantry Division, as denoted by the blue and white square insignia stuck on both sides of his helmet.

SPECIAL FEATURES

Uniform
The uniform comprises a simple green open-necked jacket and plain trousers. The single-breasted jacket has only two breast pocket flaps, simple cuffs, and no epaulettes. The later issue polyurethane helmet has side pins and a black polyurethane strap.

Also included is a pair of high brown boots similar to those issued with the US Marine in the Internationals series.

Webbing and equipment
Plate 101.1 gives some detail of the sand coloured 1941 pattern webbing. Note the link at the top of the inverted 'V' above the First Issue pattern bayonet with its plain olive green scabbard. Also shown are numerous examples of the First Issue pattern Ammo Box.

Browning .30 calibre Machine Gun
Plate 101.2 illustrates the Browning .30 M1914A4 machine gun. Moulded in black plastic, instead of silver, this simplified piece has a fixed tripod with brace between the two longest legs and a separate small leg (a marked contrast to the moveable wire and collar arrangements on the First Issue version seen in Plate 9.1). The cradle is moulded to the original pattern. There are no markings or inscriptions on this piece.

101.2

101. US MACHINE GUNNER

101.1

102. 7.62MM GP

QUARTERMASTER

- machine gun
- ammunition
- tripod
- ammo box
- sandbags

SPECIAL FEATURES

This Action Man piece is made from six pieces of olive drab plastic held together by three small Phillips screws. The three-piece tripod and cradle allow the gun to be angled and revolved. There are no markings or inscriptions on any piece of the gun.

Two AA batteries are held in the larger version of the ammunition box, a basic US piece from the First Issue Bivouac Set. The ammo box is made from three pieces of plastic and the batteries were inserted by taking off the side plate. Wired to the body of the gun, these batteries drive a cog in the body of the weapon making the loop of black polyurethane bullets rotate and lighting up a small red bulb at the end of the barrel. These effects are started by pulling back the trigger and handle at the base of the gun. Out of proportion in order to accommodate the mechanism, the gun itself is based on another Belgian FN model, the MAG, which is used by numerous countries including Britain (where it is designated the L7A1). Both plates provide a full view of this 7.62mm General Purpose weapon. Note the upright position of the rear sight in Plate 102.2.

Uniform
This British machine gun is operated by an infantryman in a late issue basic soldier's uniform. The uniform was based on plain green trousers with a rectangular pocket on the left thigh with a pointed flap, standard black ankle boots, a green nylon V necked ribbed jumper, green nylon scarf and plain green beret with a black four-cord elastic hatband.

102.2

102. 7.62MM GP

102.1

103. LEWIS GUN

103.1

SPECIAL FEATURES

The original 27lb 'light' weapon was extremely bulky. Developed by the Americans in 1911 the Mk 1 model was covered by a substantial air cooling jacket which significantly added to its weight and its size. Large quantities were made in Britain under licence by the BSA (Birmingham Small Arms) Company. The circular drum held 47 rounds of .303 ammunition.

This plate shows the circular drum at the top of the Action Man piece together with the long black polyurethane strap and moveable bipod. The gunner is dressed in a late issue British Infantryman's uniform. In colour it resembles the First Issue sets, although the material is thinner and of similar weight to the later brown versions. Note the weave on the material. The Tommy also wears a leather jerkin from the Dispatch Rider's Set (see Plate 56.1) and the standard, netting covered Mk II steel helmet.

104. GENERAL ELECTRIC SIX-PAK MINIGUN

104.1

SPECIAL FEATURES

Developed by the US General Electric Company in the 1970's, the original of the minigun was able to fire 4,000 5.56mm rounds per minute and its six barrels are powered by an electric motor. This weapon was used extensively in Vietnam, particularly in helicopter gunships.

The Action Man model in Plate 104.1 is based on this ground version and is mounted on a late issue tripod. Moulded from olive green plastic, it has two black painted pistol grips and a separately moulded and black painted sight. The tripod pin fits straight into a single moulded mount on the gun and the tripod itself is based on the same late issue pattern as the US Machine gunner piece illustrated in Plate 101.2. A separate short leg is fitted by a pin into the cradle.

Also shown in this plate is a late issue pale green Equipment Centre version of the standard camouflage two piece uniform, which does not have any breast pockets, or flaps. Note the weave on the material and the black polyurethane bullet belt.

105. RUSSIAN KALISHNIKOV PK

SPECIAL FEATURES

The Armoury series weapon shown here is a standard Russian heavy machine gun developed as part of the Kalisnikov family. The Action Man piece is a faithful reproduction, moulded in dark blue plastic with separate brown wood-grained plastic parts – namely the hollow butt, handle and pistol grip. Also shown is the black polyurethane bi-pod and bullet belt, the latter unique to this piece.

Plate 105.2 is a close up of the weapon, a standard Russian green and silver ammunition box, and a 1941 pattern helmet.

The late Equipment Centre version of the Paratroop Regiment pattern camouflage uniform can be seen in Plate 105.1 with its lighter green and brown colouring.

105. RUSSIAN KALISHNIKOV PK MACHINE GUN

105.1

106. SIG 510-4

SPECIAL FEATURES

This Swiss SIG 510-4 rifle is included in the SAS Assault Craft Set (see Plate 91.1). It was also issued on later Action Man carded equipment issues, for example The Armoury series, and themed Weapons Arsenal cards such as Nato Night Manoeuvres.

The Action Man piece is moulded in dark blue plastic with a painted red-brown butt. This version includes a telescopic sight and a large separate night vision disc with a red paper sticker lens, which was connected to the body of the piece by a single cord of black elastic. The standard Action Man bipod shown here can be folded down from its front lug. Also pictured is a late variant of the Royal Marines Arctic Warfare Set uniform.

106.1

107. LATE ISSUE PONCHO

107.1

SPECIAL FEATURES

One of the last remaining First Issue pieces to survive onto a Quartermasters Stores card. This plate shows a later poncho; cut to the original pattern it is made of a thinner material than the First Issue, but is still water proof.

108. SECOND ISSUE COMBAT JACKET

QUARTERMASTER

Separate Armoury Card:
- M-16
- bipod
- camouflaged field telephone

SPECIAL FEATURES

Included with all Second Issue Action Soldiers is a simplified version of the combat jacket (based on the original Combat piece in Plate 2.1). This version is fastened by two poppers, instead of a zip, and also dispenses with the separately fastened cuffs and epaulettes. There are belt loops at each side of the waist. Also included are a plain pair of green trousers with square open back pockets, standard black ankle boots. A dark blue version of the first pattern of beret with a silver star and crown badge completes this uniform.

108.1

Also shown is the camouflaged version of the First Issue field telephone and the bipod version of the M16. These were included in some later equipment cards, such as the Armoury or Equipment Centre series. The handset connects to the field telephone with thin black tubing, instead of the single-cord elastic used in the First Issue pieces. There is a Hasbro inscription on the top of the headset box.

109. LAST ISSUE CAMOUFLAGE

SPECIAL FEATURES

Armed with a Baretta pistol in dark blue plastic, the figure in Plate 109.1 is dressed in a late issue camouflage uniform which was of a significantly different quality and hue to its predecessors. The material has a more synthetic appearance and is stitched with nylon thread. This uniform is based on the Second Issue pattern with pointed breast pocket flaps only. Note the open neck and poppers.

The kepi style cap is similar to those included in the First Issue Action Soldier and Action Pilot sets. The set of wings at the front are embossed onto the plastic and then filled with silver paint. This style of kepi appears in several late issue catalogues, and there are also brown and blue versions.

110. ASSAULT CRAFT

QUARTERMASTER

- **assault craft**
- **outboard motor**
- **paddle**
- **rope**

SPECIAL FEATURES

An example of the moulded green hard polyurethane type of Assault Craft, it includes a working electric outboard motor. This is of similar design to that included with the Jungle Explorer Rivercraft, but all in green and with an extended moulded handle. On the floor of the dingy are the two black plastic oars, a sledgehammer, green rope and the post War Belgian FN L4A2 Light Machine Gun (shown here with a straight magazine and its bi-pod extended).

The Royal Marine in this plate is wearing a Quartermaster's Stores era green duffel coat made from a 'woolly' textured synthetic material. The coat fastens at the front with two poppers and features a simple hood, two open square pockets and three chestnut coloured plastic toggles. The second pattern green beret, with an incongruous Royal Tank Regiment badge, is also included.

110.1

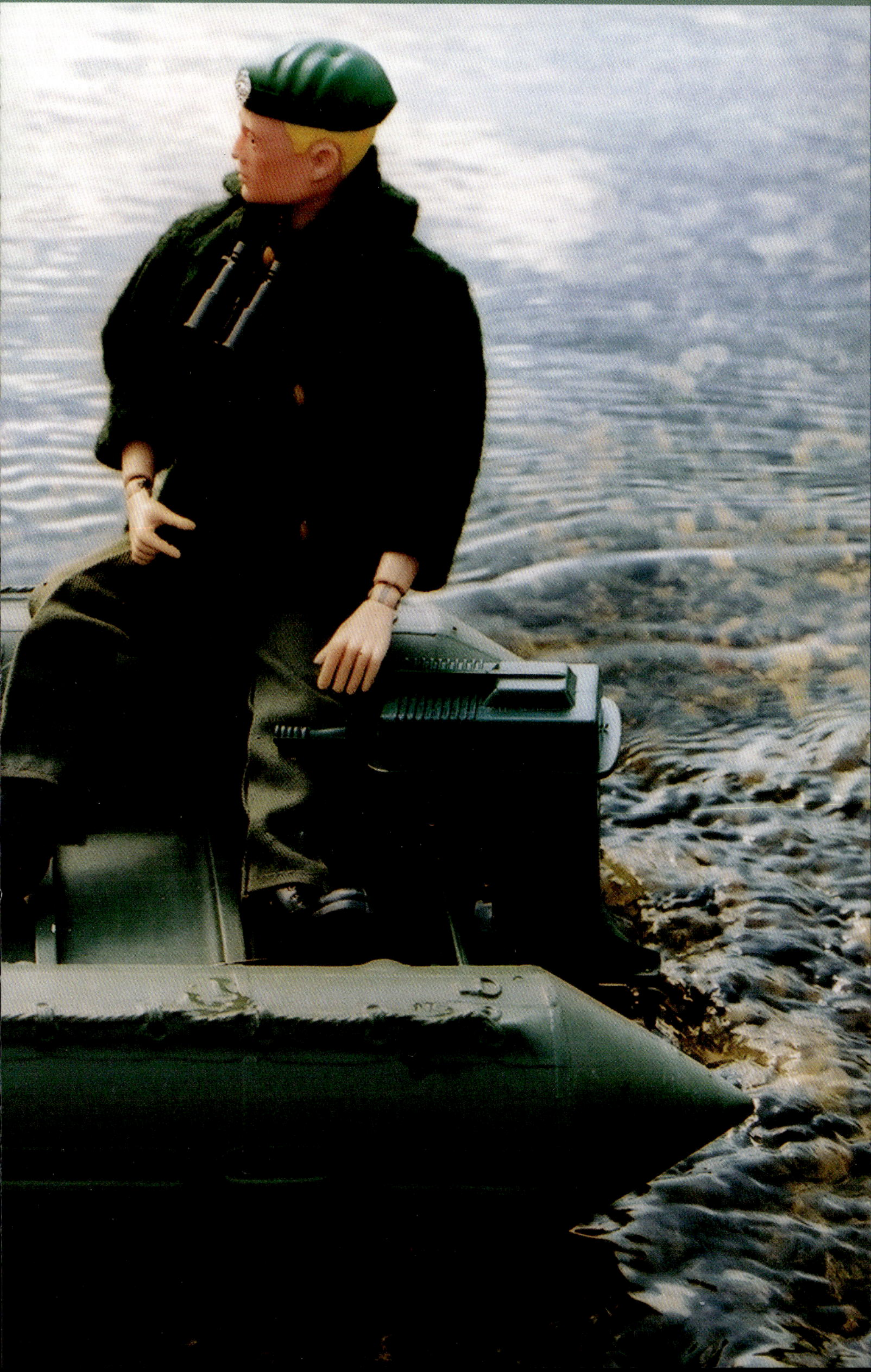

111. HIGH RESCUE

QUARTERMASTER

- hardhat
- overalls
- boots
- chainsaw
- chest winch

SPECIAL FEATURES

Part of the later Emergency Series, this all yellow one-piece suit is a simpler version of the original one-piece pattern. Plain, without elasticated cuffs or half waist, it has three popper fasteners instead of the zip.

Also included in this set is the yellow peaked hard hat with a central white stripe. The white and silver painted plastic chainsaw can be seen in Plate 111.1. There are no markings and inscriptions on any of these pieces.

NOT SHOWN:
the somewhat impractical yellow plastic chest winch.

111. HIGH RESCUE

111.1

112. LATE ISSUE M3

SPECIAL FEATURES

Plate 112.1 shows three examples of later issue equipment: the blue version of the winged motif kepi, the blue one-piece boiler suit included in the Go-Kart Set and an all-silver version of the Saboteur's M-3 machine pistol with a black polyurethane strap. There are no markings and inscriptions on either this piece or the kepi.

113. UNDERGROUND RESCUE

QUARTERMASTER

- miner's hat with lamp
- overall
- boots
- pic axe
- hammer
- rope
- pitons
- karibiners
- storm lamp

SPECIAL FEATURES

These plates illustrate an orange late issue version of the one-piece suit. Again it has three poppers and simple cuffs, but retains the elasticated half waist. Included in this set is a white polyurethane pit helmet with a red lamp – note the late pin and polyurethane strap design.

Other parts of the set are the storm lamp, ice pick, hammer, karibiners and pitons. The high eight-eyelet boots are a rarity for such a late issue set, when ankle boots were the norm.

113. UNDERGROUND RESCUE

113.1

114. HIGHWAY HAZARD

QUARTERMASTER

- roveralls
- boots
- vest
- axewire cutters
- fire extinguisher
- jack

Workshop Accessories:
- toolbox
- drill
- pliers
- screwdriver
- hammer
- spanner
- hazard cones
- petrol can
- jack
- sledgehammer
- pick axe
- shovel
- hand crane

SPECIAL FEATURES

Overalls
This navy blue one-piece suit is distinguished by a diagonal zip, which fastens from hip to neck, and two silver strips on the sleeves.

Equipment Vest
The yellow PVC equipment vest is based on a late issue life vest, with its thinner straps and Made in Hong Kong inscription on the bottom seal. Note the four tool loops across the middle of the vest.

Toolbox and Tools
Also shown are the two orange plastic traffic cones with their white paper rings and the yellow and silver jack (which can be raised by turning the square bit in the revolving cog mechanism). The blue grey tool box holds the screwdriver, blue handled pliers and spanner and is moulded from one piece of polyurethane which is clipped together by two pins on each flap. Inside is a black tray, with pins to keep the hammer and an orange coloured plastic drill in place. Also shown here are the sledgehammer, jerrycan, silver plastic version of the wire cutters, shovel, pickaxe, red axe and small fire extinguisher. Some workshop accessories came on a separate card to the overalls and equipment vest.

114.2

114. HIGHWAY HAZARD

114.1

115. 27TH CAVALRY

QUARTERMASTER

- kepi
- scarf
- shirt
- breeches
- braces
- riding boots
- spurs
- belt and holster
- pistol
- sword and scabbard

115.1

SPECIAL FEATURES

Part of a Wild West series, which included a Cowboy Scout and two types of Indian - a Brave and a Chief - Plate 115.1 shows the 7th Cavalry outfit. Some detail of the sergeant's uniform can be seen, notably the three yellow fabric stripes. The single-breasted navy blue jacket has five golden spike buttons. Fastened by two poppers this jacket has a closed collar with separate cuffs but no epaulettes. The kepi is made of navy coloured polyurethane with a painted peak and painted gold buttons at either side of the hatband. A metal '7th Cavalry' badge is pinned into the front.

The unique shape of the calf length boots is shown in Plate 115.2 together with the chromed spurs. Unlike other Action Man pieces, these go all the way around the ankle and are fitted under the heel with a polyurethane strap. Also clearly shown in this Plate is the separate waistband on the trousers, the denim reinforced seat, and yellow leg stripes.

115. 27TH CAVALRY

The yellow braces fit, using elastic loops, onto buttons on the waist of the sky blue trousers. Around the neck is a simple triangular yellow cotton scarf made of the same material as the braces.

Note the size of the pistol with its black painted handle and black polyurethane holster belt. Only the holster and bullets were moulded on to the belt; the strap for the scabbard is a separate piece threaded over the scabbard and looped around the belt. Also shown is the standard pattern Action Man cavalry sword, derived from the earlier Ceremonial series it has a black grip, chromed guard and plain plastic blade.